MANNA

MANNA

the call to daily dependence on God

KEVIN STIRRATT

BEACON HILL PRESS

OF KANSAS CITY

Copyright 2009 by Kevin Stirratt and
Beacon Hill Press of Kansas City

ISBN 978-0-8341-2432-5

Printed in the
United States of America

Cover Design: Arthur Cherry
Internal Design: Sharon Page

Library of Congress Cataloging-in-Publication Data

Stirratt, Kevin, 1967-
    Manna : the call to daily dependence on God / Kevin Stirratt.
        p. cm.
    Includes bibliographical references.
    ISBN 978-0-8341-2432-5 (pbk.)
    1. Trust in God—Christianity. I. Title.

    BV4637.S74 2009
    248.4—dc22

                                                    2008055719

10 9 8 7 6 5 4 3 2 1

CONTENTS

ACKNOWLEDGMENTS

I want to thank the many people who have worked hard to bring this manuscript to publication. Joyce Poeppelmeyer, Darrell Poeppelmeyer, Nancy Kupfersmith, Michaelle Stirratt, and Rosalie Stirratt provided valuable insights and questions that took this work to a level I could not have dreamed possible.

To my wife, Diana, and my boys, Andrew and Daniel, I offer more than thanks. Your patience and sacrifice of countless hours allowed me to give the attention necessary to take what God has been teaching all of us and put it into written form.

I also want to thank the staff at Segue Foundation, who believed enough in the value of this material to allow me the time to finish it. Your belief, encouragement, and support are so very much appreciated.

To Bonnie Perry and the publishing team at Beacon Hill Press, I offer my sincerest gratitude for your immediate belief in and support for this work. Your confidence was a confirmation of God's call to write *Manna*.

Finally, I want to thank God for trusting me enough to allow me to endure the days of trial in which He was opening up to my understanding the joyful growth of daily dependence. He is my shelter and my rock.

INTRODUCTION

"Give us today our daily bread." This beautiful prayer leads us to undertake the most terrifying spiritual journey of all—living a life of absolute dependence on the miraculous hand of God. Many times we have said things such as, "I wish God would show me miracles today!" We love the idea of experiencing the miraculous. But are we prepared for the treacherous journey of living on manna?

Taking seriously Jesus' instructions to pray like this means seeking to be as dependent on God as were the children of Israel on their journey through the desert. Manna was God's provision. The Israelites had to collect it every day and only enough for that day. In fact, if they gathered more than one day's provision, maggots would infest the excess. Having our needs supplied this way sounds wonderful: "I don't have to cook today; God is going to provide. I don't have to do anything but get up and expect God to come through."

But think about it. That also means every night we must go to bed and ask ourselves if we really do trust God to come through. Every night we must go to bed with bare cupboards, an empty refrigerator, and no backup plan. If God doesn't come through in the morning, we will starve.

Our peace in that kind of a relationship is totally dependent on our faith. Do we really believe God is there? Does He really care about us? Can we really trust Him to not lose focus on us and our needs? When we open the front door in the morning, can we really trust that God has provided once again, not an overabundance, but just enough to make it through the day?

Yes, we call out for a life full of miracles. But we would prefer to be in the crowd *observing* the miracle. We really do not want to be the paralytic or the leper. What we really want is to be entertained by the miracles of God when what we need is to be transformed by them.

And so here is the call to transformation—to become absolutely dependent on God and to live trusting Him for our daily provision. Is it enough for us to know that God is going to provide, or do we demand He show us what tomorrow holds before we begin the journey? Can we enter into days of scarcity with a sense of security and provision that aren't dependent on a huge bank account or an overabundance of reserves? Do we trust that God is our only true provision?

When God's presence is enough for us to trust His provision, He is able to begin using us in ways He could never have done before. Where the risk for others would be too great, we are able to step into the river, believing it will divide. Where others see giants, we see a land God has already given us. When others see an impenetrable fortress, we sound the trumpets and watch God destroy the strongholds of our enemy. God has called us to this level of trust because it is one of the foundations He uses to change our world through us. Living on daily bread, manna, is a wonderful, frightening journey of absolute dependence, where the miracles of God are a daily blessing.

As you explore the pages to come, a study guide has been provided at the end of the book. The study guide questions will help you explore your own spiritual journey as you are learning to trust God for daily bread.

◢ 1 LIVING ON MANNA
The Call to Daily Dependence

This, then, is how you should pray. . . . "Give us today our daily bread" (Matt. 6:9, 11).

Learning Daily Dependence

Living on manna is a wonderful, yet frightening, journey on which we learn to trust God for our daily provision. It isn't a journey we complete. It is a daily journey of praying again and again, "Give us today our daily bread."

My wife and I had been in ministry just long enough to learn a few things and not long enough to learn what we needed to know—that we didn't know anything. We had served under the leadership of two very gifted pastors who were gracious enough to shield us from the criticism young pastors often face.

With the experience came arrogance. I was convinced I was ready to lead. I was ready to take on a challenge and impress people with my being "such a young and wise leader." But God had something else in mind. He was about to take me into the desert to teach me what it means to live on manna.

We packed up the truck and headed west. My ten-month-old son sat in his car seat between me and my wife as we towed our car behind the U-haul. South Dakota, look out! Your savior is coming. Little did I know the lesson God had in store for me.

The church was young, less than three years old, and had been planted by one of the most gracious, loving pastors I have met. He knew people and loved them more deeply than I ever could. But I was too naive to know it and too big for my own britches to admit it if I had.

I had $6,000 in the bank but hadn't learned to surrender any of it to God. After six years of ministry I had only recently begun to give a true tithe. I had "tipped" God for years. I treated Him like an IRS tax return. I looked for every reason to avoid giving so much. The testimony of a board member about moving from tithing on his net income to tithing on his gross income was a turning point, and I began to trust God with my money.

However, I was far from learning the true daily trust of living on manna.

The first months were horrible. Rather than the 85 we had been told were attending that fledgling church, we began with 15 our first Sunday and the situation didn't get any better. The church had been receiving $5,000 a month support from our denominational leadership. Those funds dwindled to $500 within a year. Our child care costs skyrocketed to over $1,000 a month. Our $6,000 in the bank quickly turned to thousands of dollars of debt.

I was learning a very hard lesson—I needed God. I didn't just need Him a little. I needed Him more desperately than I could ever have believed. I needed Him when I woke up, and I needed Him when I lay down. I needed Him when I was asleep. Like Jacob, I had started the journey convinced I was blessed, but now I was sleeping with my head on a rock and I needed God to intervene in a miraculous way.

I will never forget the night I finally broke. I had tried to encourage a board member to make some changes in her leadership style the day before. These were changes I didn't want to bring up, but I knew that this person and the church would be harmed if they were not made. I was at the bottom of my emotional barrel. Our church met in a school, and my basement seconded as my office. A board meeting was scheduled to meet in thirty minutes, and board members would be showing up any time. I remember hearing the first footsteps on the porch and wondering why they didn't ring the bell. I went to open the door to find a plastic grocery bag hanging on the doorknob.

I had been working tirelessly to teach leadership principles to my new board. I had given each board member a pile of material to take home and look over in his or her spare time. I quickly recognized the contents in the plastic bag. It was the material I had given the board member I had tried to spur on. My heart sank. She wasn't going to follow my leadership. My sense of failure was crushing.

The package contained a scathing letter accusing me of everything from legalism to being young. As I read the letter, I lay across my desk and wept in prayer, asking God for help. In that moment I let go of all pretense. I was no great leader. I was a kid playing grown-up in a very difficult world. I was arrogant but had no skills to back it up. For all my book knowledge, I was lacking what these people needed. I wasn't their resource. God was. I wasn't my family's resource. God was. And in those moments of desperation, I begged God just to get me through that night. "Give me what I need to breathe for a few minutes." I had quit managing tomorrow and had desperately fallen on my face before God for just enough sustenance to get through today.

I was learning what Jesus meant when He called us to pray for "daily bread."

As painful as it was, it was the beginning of the most freeing spiritual journey of my life. I was learning to live on manna. I was learning that I didn't control tomorrow and that I didn't have any resource to count on other than God. God's presence and His provision for today were going to have to be sufficient for me to trust Him with the journey.

Dependent on Miracles

When Jesus taught the disciples to pray in Matt. 6, He told them to pray, "Give us today our daily bread." That's wonderful when it is taken as just a poetic sentiment intended to elevate our understanding of a gracious God. But it is an entirely different matter when God allows us to face the terrifying reality of *needing* daily bread. And yet, during those times God can use such harsh realities to begin a transformation in our hearts that will free us to trust Him beyond our circumstances.

Jesus is reminding us of the kind of absolute dependence on the miraculous hand of God that the children of Israel had to accept in order to survive the harsh realities of their journey to the Promised Land. They had left Egypt. As horrific as the conditions in Egypt had been, the Israelites were at least provided some kind of nourishment. But in the desert, there was no captor to feed them. There was no one but God.

Only a couple of months had gone by on the Israelites' journey before they ran out of resources and began to panic. "It would have been better if we had just stayed in Egypt. We're going to starve if we keep following You." (See Exod. 14:12.) I realize it is tempting to take a self-righteous stand here and accuse the Israelites of having little faith. After all, this group had just witnessed the Passover. God had freed them as no army ever could, and He had struck down the firstborn of all those who refused to become a part of this family of faith. Through a series of miraculous plagues, and now through the stunning display of ultimate authority, God had delivered them from a captor they couldn't defeat. They had seen the mighty hand of God and were now complaining that He was not able to care for them on the very journey He had ordained.

Before we lower the gavel and pass judgment, we must take a look at our own lives and honestly admit we have much in common with the children of Israel. We know the hand of God. He has performed miracle upon miracle in our lives. And yet, when faced with the harsh realities of life and the truth that we don't have what we think we need, we are just as prone to begin accusing God of falling short on His end of the bargain: "After all I have sacrificed, I can't believe You'd let me go through this!"

We are all very fortunate that God is gracious and patient. He provided a solution for the Israelites, and that solution is a pattern for us to follow. God's solution was manna. He provided for the needs of the Israelites, not through huge storehouses of grain and meat, but through the daily provision of "just enough."

For forty years the Israelites would experience a daily miracle. God would provide manna for them to eat. Every morning they awoke to find God's provision of wonderful bread with the taste of honey. Each family was to gather enough to eat in a day. They were not to gather more than a day's supply except for the day before the Sabbath. They would be required to trust God each and every day for the provision.

This is where the most difficult emotional decision comes into play. Do we trust God with tomorrow? Can we really believe that just because He provided for us today, He is going to come through again in the morning? After all, our very lives are on the line here! If God doesn't come through, we're going to starve.

And so the temptation becomes real and vicious. We reason that it is wise to gather as much as we can, just in case God fails us. We enjoy provision. But we detest *daily* provision. We love it when God pours out so many blessings on us that we don't have room enough for them (see Mal. 3). We just don't like it when He pours out those blessings one day at a time.

This is at the heart of Jesus' instructions. Pray for the ability to trust the Blessing Giver more than the blessings. Enjoy the blessings. Praise God for the blessings. But never replace your trust in the Blessing Giver with a trust in the blessings. This whole spiritual journey is about learning that we are safe regardless of the circumstances. We must learn that the miracles of God come in daily portions and that we don't have to have what we need for tomorrow to know He is going to take care of tomorrow. We must learn the trust of daily provision.

No Reserves

Trusting in God's daily provision means refusing to trust in reserves. Some of the children of Israel gathered more than a day's provision. Hoarding manna just in case God failed was an incredible slap in God's face. Like Abraham, the children of Israel were trying to create an Ishmael—a plan B. "Just in case You don't provide the way to fulfill Your promises, God, I'm going to create a plan B as a backup." The extra manna of the Israelites rotted and filled with maggots. This is the destiny of all our plan Bs.

We are all tempted at this point. We discover God's will for our lives and look at the risks involved. While we may never admit it, we ask the honest question, "What if God fails me?" "What will I need to stay safe if God doesn't come through?" And then we start gathering the resources we need for our back-up plan. And when we have finally gathered enough, we look at God and say, "I'm ready!"

The problem is we aren't usable when we need a plan B to be safe. God can't use us until we are willing to follow Him into the unknown. In order to use us to transform the world around us, God needs us absolutely dependent on Him. He needs us to let go of whatever crutches we are leaning on and shift the weight of our trust onto His faithfulness. Jesus is calling us to pray for a kind of faith that doesn't need a pile of reserves before we are willing to begin the journey.

Whatever journey God is calling you to, waking up to His daily provision will either be terrifying or invigorating. A part of us says, "Wow! Wouldn't it be amazing to wake up and find manna on the lawn? Wouldn't it be wonderful to live every day experiencing the miraculous hand of God?" And yet, we must remember that to live that way also means being willing to go to bed at night with nothing left in the proverbial cupboards. The resources for today, as precious as they were, are gone. In the end, our money, our prestige, our energy, our abilities—all of it means nothing. And we have to go to bed tonight making a decision of faith: "Do we trust God to come through tomorrow?"

If we can finally break through to this spiritual victory and savor the prayer, "Give us today our daily bread," then the morning becomes something to anticipate rather than to dread. We don't walk out the front door wondering whether God came through. We walk out expecting to see what God has done today to meet our needs. It changes the way we deal with adversity and scarcity. We are no longer at risk. We may not know how God is going to provide, but we do know He is going to do it.

What Do We Want—Entertainment or Transformation?

If we are going to be able to make this spiritual transformation to living on God's daily provision, we have got to make up our minds about what we want from God. How many times have we said things such as, "If only I could see a miracle, I would believe," or "God, just show me a miracle and I will follow You." We all want to see the miracles of God. We just don't want to *need* the miracle.

Although we are going to explore this topic more deeply in chapter 5, right now we need to recognize one of the major areas that keep us from embracing God's provision: What we really want is to be entertained by the miracles of God when what we need is to be transformed by them.

We enjoy watching God perform miracles. We just don't want to be the blind man or the leper. We want to stand on the sidelines where there is no risk. But we don't want to be the lame man who lived for decades begging for food. We want to be a spectator in the grandstands cheering our team to victory. But we really don't want to know the pain of need.

But Jesus is calling us to accept God's design for our spiritual transformation. We can be entertained on the sidelines, but we can only experience God's miraculous power when our absolute need for Him is revealed and we cry out for help. To pray for daily bread is to welcome every part of the journey God leads us through—even the painful parts. Those are the times when we look with expectation: "God, what are You going to show me through this? How are You going to transform me? How will Your miraculous hand provide a way of escape here? How is my faith going to be stretched during these days in the wilderness?"

We must learn dependence for today. We must learn to trust God for tomorrow. And in this "daily bread" kind of faith, we must learn that our need is simply the pathway through which God will deliver His miracle. If we are to experience His hand, we are going to *need* His hand. And so regardless of the kind of blessings He pours out on us, we must choose to trust God, not the blessings. We must refuse to allow our trust in God to be determined by the abundance of the provision. We must also refuse to curse God because we are in want. Instead, we must embrace our need for God, no matter how He delivers His blessings.

One Provider

Getting to the place where we trust God more than His blessings will require that we hold on to God as our only provider. In the same way the children of Israel had no other resource to provide for them, we must place God in our hearts and minds as the one true resource of our lives.

We are tempted to trust our money, our abilities, our relationships, and a host of other things to keep us safe. They are the things we turn to when we are in trouble. We are in fact creating idols out of those resources. We trust them for our safety and turn to them as our first line of defense. But to live on manna means to refuse to buy into the myth that anything other than God has the ability to keep us safe.

We will deal with this further in chapter 3. But for now, we must admit to ourselves that we do not always trust God more than our money, our wisdom, our abilities, our families, and so on. We don't turn to God first when we are in trouble. We each have a host of resources that we would prefer to rely on instead of God. And God wants to see that change.

This is a mental battle we fight in times of plenty and want. When there is an overabundance of resources to meet our needs, we are tempted to trust the resources more than the God who provided them. When there seem to be too few resources, we are tempted to accuse God of losing sight of our needs and not paying the kind of attention we expect.

When we choose to pray, "Give us today our daily bread," we choose to believe God is going to come through. We refuse to accept what we see around us: "There isn't enough time, money, energy, love, forgiveness, whatever! But somehow, someway, God is going to provide! I'm not going to panic. Yes, I am going to pray fervently and call out to God with everything I have. But it isn't because I doubt His ability. It is because I am convinced He is the only one I can trust to take care of this!" The cry of our heart is one of expectation, not accusation. He will come through. We are joining our prayer of faith with God's desire to be our provider.

The Questions We Must Answer

If we are going to break through to this spiritual victory of daily dependence, living on manna, there are some fundamental questions we must answer.

Is God really there? This is the question of *belief.* Do we really believe God is here and cares about our needs? Do we really believe He is going to come through? If we do, it will change the way we deal with the realities and difficulties of life. Peace really can be the norm for our lives, even in the middle of chaos, scarcity, and uncertainty.

What keeps me safe? This is the question of *provision.* Until we make up our minds that God alone is our provider, we will not be willing to risk absolute trust in God's provision. We must move beyond a limited faith based on what we can see, to a deep faith based on God's presence. What sources of safety have become gods in our lives? In what ways do we need to shift our trust in these other sources of safety back to God?

Is enough for today enough for me? This is the question of *values.* What do we value most? Has materialism choked out our ability to experience the deep level of trust modeled in living on manna? Do we need God to show us tomorrow before we will agree to join Him on the journey? Are we willing to live in scarcity if He leads us down that path? Is our trust in God dependent on the level of abundance He provides, or can we agree to follow the One who has no place to lay His head?

Do I want entertainment or transformation? We have to make up our minds whether we are going to be spectators or participants in the miracles of God. Do we want transformation in our lives so much that we are willing to allow God to take us into dangerous territory? We must walk with Him through "the valley of the shadow of death" (Ps. 23:4) for us to really know there is no need to fear evil. We can watch others take that journey from afar, but we can only become more like Him if we are willing to endure the trials that lead to transformation.

The chapters to come will lead us through this amazing journey into absolute dependence on the miraculous hand of God. We will look closely at these questions. When we break through and come to the end of our self-sufficiency and our need to possess tomorrow before we follow God today, we will find His answer to our questions.

The answer is provision, and it is as sweet as honey. We are able to be used by God to transform the world around us, because we are willing to risk trusting God's capacity to provide. We don't need to see tomorrow to walk into it. We don't have to possess the blessing to know it is being poured out on us. This is the kind of faith God uses to part the waters and drop the walls of Jericho. We are ready to experience the blessings of God without the temptation to shift our worship away from the Blessing Giver. Peace is no longer dependent on the circumstances around us but on the God who is in us.

As you explore the pages to come and ask the fundamental questions of living on manna, I want to invite you to an honest conversation with God. Allow Him to dig deep and to reveal to you those places in your relationship with Him where He wants to transform your heart and deepen your dependency on His ability to provide.

2 THE QUESTION OF BELIEF

Is God Really There?

As I was with Moses, so I will be with you; I will never leave you nor forsake you (Josh. 1:5).

Is God There, and Does He Care?

If we are going to be able to live out Jesus' call to pray "Give us today our daily bread," we must first settle the question of belief: "Is God really there, and more importantly, does He really care about me?" To put it more plainly, "Who's got my back, God or me?" It isn't an accident that within a few verses of the Lord's Prayer, Jesus instructs us with the following:

> [25]Therefore I tell you, do not worry about your life, what you will eat or drink; or about your body, what you will wear. Is not life more important than food, and the body more important than clothes? [26]Look at the birds of the air; they do not sow or reap or store away in barns, and yet your heavenly Father feeds them. Are you not much more valuable than they? [27]Who of you by worrying can add a single hour to his life?
>
> [28]And why do you worry about clothes? See how the lilies of the field grow. They do not labor or spin. [29]Yet I tell you that not even Solomon in all his splendor was dressed like one of these. [30]If that is how God clothes the grass of the field, which is here today and tomorrow is thrown into the fire, will he not much more clothe you, O you of little faith? [31]So do not worry, saying, "What shall we eat?" or "What shall we drink?" or "What shall we wear?" [32]For the pagans run after all these things, and your heavenly Father knows that you need them. [33]But seek first his kingdom and his righteousness, and all these things will be given to you as well. [34]Therefore do not worry about tomorrow, for tomorrow will worry about itself. Each day has enough trouble of its own. (Matt. 6:25-34)

Jesus puts it right out there. We have to make up our minds whether we believe there is a God who cares about our needs. If we don't believe that, we will spend our lives in a state of panic:

"How am I going to get enough food to survive? What about clothes? I am out here on my own! I am going to die!"

When we make up our minds that we believe there is a God who clothes the grass of the field, causes the lilies to grow, and takes care of the birds of the air, we are brought face-to-face with the reality that God cares about us more than those things! When we are utterly convinced that the God of heaven, who keeps every part of this universe under control, is intensely concerned about us and our needs, it doesn't make sense to worry.

In fact, this issue of belief—"Do I believe there is a God who knows my needs, cares about my needs, and takes care of my needs?"—is the definitive difference between the pagan and the Christian (vv. 32-33). The pagan answers, "Nobody but me takes care of me. I am the only one I can count on. If I don't do everything in my power to take care of myself, I am dead!" And so the pagan spends his or her entire life running after "stuff." The car is never new enough. The house is never big enough. The toys are never cool enough. The paycheck is never large enough. Nothing ever reaches the point of being "enough."

I saw this firsthand working in an investment firm. I worked with men who made $250,000 a year. Some would treat each other to $500 dinners and then brag to the other brokers about their generosity. And yet, they would complain they weren't in the elite group—those who made at least $500,000 a year. They worked insane hours and would fight with each other over accounts that might boost their pay another few dollars a year. They had lost all grasp of the financial blessings they had because they just didn't understand who it is that really provides. In their minds they had to keep fighting for what they had or risk losing it all. They were running after the things that couldn't satisfy, and their overabundance was never enough.

Jesus is warning us about what happens when we refuse to maintain a proper relationship to God's blessings. When we run after the blessings instead of the Blessing Giver, we never gain peace (vv. 31-32). The blessings are never enough, and we are filled with worry.

So how do we find peace in the middle of either scarcity or abundance? We fully acknowledge the heart of our belief: "Your heavenly father knows that you need them" (v. 32). While pagans run after the blessing because their trust is in the "stuff" they possess, believers are called to seek the Blessing Giver who knows their needs. Peace comes from absolute trust in the Blessing Giver, not in the blessing.

I think this is one of the most amazing parts of Jesus' teaching. He isn't saying, "You have to stay in poverty to be blessed." He assures us that God is fully aware of what we need. He even says God will provide these things when we remain in a proper relationship with Him. But Jesus is also honest about what happens to us when we shift our worship—what we truly believe in—from the One who blesses to the blessings themselves. We become panic-ridden. And so the call is to stay aware that God is the One in whom we believe. We aren't to chase after the blessings, but after God.

This allows us to handle extreme adversity and scarcity with an honest call to God. We call out with desperate trust, not accusation: "God, I believe You are here. I want You to know *You have a problem!* I would appreciate it if You could do something about it!" I am not saying we are always perfectly at peace in these situations. But God is working with us to teach us that we can trust Him. He is helping us learn to call out to Him rather than simply panic.

A good friend of mine tells the story of one of these "God,

You have a problem" days. Her story illustrates this choice to believe in God's ability to provide. Laura and her husband, Steve, are pastors in Indiana. Steve and Laura had answered their call to ministry later in life and had sacrificed good jobs to move their kids to the outskirts of Kankakee, Illinois, to study for the ministry at Olivet Nazarene University. If anyone had a right to expect God to take care of their needs, they did.

However, God tends to pour out His blessings one day at a time, and Steve and Laura were hurting financially. They lived in an old farmhouse in the country, and they were stone broke. That morning Laura had sent the kids to school knowing there was only a quarter stick of margarine left in the refrigerator. Her prayers were a mix of anger and honest despair: "God, if You don't do something here, my kids aren't going to eat tonight." The more she prayed, the angrier she got. "God, You called us here. We sacrificed to follow what You told us to do!" She prayed and fussed until finally Laura's "in your face" personality let it all fly.

She grabbed a piece of paper and a pen and started making out her grocery list. "God, You said You would provide, so I am going to tell you what I would like for You to provide!" Laura started writing out a grocery list for God. She mentally went up and down the grocery aisle pulling items into her imaginary cart. Flour, sugar, cooking oil—they all went on her list. She didn't just stay with the staples either. She wanted cookies and chocolate chips too! Item after item were transferred from her heart to the paper until her grocery list was complete. And then, with stubborn faith, Laura took a magnet and placed her grocery list on the front of the refrigerator. "There, God! Now what are You going to do about that?" Malachi 3 calls us to "Test me in this . . ." Laura had done just that!

Laura and Steve lived a little over two hours away from their home church in Havana, Illinois. An hour and a half after her desperate cry to God, Laura heard the sound of a car coming down the gravel lane. She peeked out the window to see some of her church family piling out of a car. "What in the world?" And then the Great Provider smiled at His sense of humor as those dear people started pulling grocery bags from the trunk. One by one they hauled in the manna and placed it on Laura's table.

Laura told them about her tirade with God, and they began checking off her grocery list together. There were the choco-late chips. There were the cookies. One by one every item was checked off. Everything was there except for cooking oil, so one of the ladies gave Laura five dollars to buy oil. They rejoiced at God's handiwork and laughed at the arrogance that would even begin to accuse God of not taking care of His children. They all were affirmed with this truth: "God has our back!"

The church ladies had been gathering food for some time and in God's ordained timing had been on the road before Laura had even begun writing down her list. The next Sunday those dear ladies stood in the church service to testify to God's provi-sion. One lady who hadn't made the trip to Steve and Laura's stood up with tears in her eyes. "I had the oil and I forgot it!"

God's provision had begun weeks before Steve and Laura knew they would have a need. God was teaching them and their children something about the God who clothes the grass of the field. He knows your need before you ever could. His atten-tion isn't diverted by the complexity of our circumstances. He isn't panicked by the severity of our need. His resources aren't stretched by our apparent poverty. He knows what our needs are, and He cares more about us than anything else He has cre-ated (v. 26).

Laura was able to turn her desperation into an act of faith because she had a core belief that God was there. She didn't rebel against God, even in the "You've got a problem!" approach of her prayer. She was honest and up front with God. This is the first step to answering the question of belief—we must move from a fairytale belief in God to a gut-level belief.

Moving Beyond Fairytale Faith

I grew up in the church. I heard the stories about Jesus from the very early days of my life. When I heard the stories of Jonah and the whale, Noah and the ark, and Daniel and the lions' den, God was painting the backdrop for my own faith journey. But I still had to come to the place in my life where I chose to believe that God still does the miraculous.

Many of us accept these stories on a kind of religious level that rejects miracles as a possibility in today's world. I have even heard people ask, "Why doesn't God perform miracles anymore?" They are quite surprised when I say, "He does!" Their confused looks give away their disbelief. For many of us, the miracles of God rank right up there with "Jack and the Beanstalk" or "Snow White." They teach wonderful lessons. But they don't really speak of reality. God is someone that we accept on a "religious" level but not as an active participant in our daily lives: "I will pray to Him and hope it helps. But don't expect me to trust Him to take care of me—that's my job." Unwittingly, we take the posture of the pagan instead of the posture of the believer: "I trust in *me*. I am god."

To pray "Give us today our daily bread" is to accept once and for all that God is real and that He cares enough about us to know our needs and provide. This one truth is a core foundation of how we should deal with adversity and scarcity: "God doesn't lose His focus on me!"

You and I might feel insignificant in a world filled with problems more severe than our own. Often we even feel guilty about "bothering" God with our small issues. "There are people dying of AIDS in Africa. How can I bother God with this?" But we must choose to believe in a God whose capacity to focus on us isn't diminished by the needs of our neighbor. His resources aren't limited. He can meet both your needs *and* the needs of others without ever depleting His storehouse. We choose to believe in a God with unlimited resources and an unlimited ability to focus on each and every person all at the same time.

Belief Changes How We Handle Adversity

When we have fully trusted that God is real, cares about us, and never loses His focus on us, it changes how we handle adversity. It isn't that we enjoy trials—not at all. However, our cries to God move from anxiety to anticipation. Paul talked about this transformation in Rom. 5:1-5:

Therefore, since we have been justified through faith, we have peace with God through our Lord Jesus Christ, through whom we have gained access by faith into this grace in which we now stand. And we rejoice in the hope of the glory of God. Not only so, but we also rejoice in our sufferings, because we know that suffering produces perseverance; perseverance, character; and character, hope. And hope does not disappoint us, because God has poured out his love into our hearts by the Holy Spirit, whom he has given us.

Paul is teaching us about the peace we have with God because we have received forgiveness. God has proved His love for us in that He died for us before we ever asked for help. He provided what we most desperately needed before we even admitted our need. In the middle of this Paul teaches the proper understanding about adversity and suffering. He tells us that suffering produces perseverance, which produces character, which produces hope.

Let me explain. When we are new to our faith and deal with the adversities of life, we often feel we aren't going to make it. We cry out to God with the kind of desperation that screams, "If You don't come through here, I am going to die!" God provides time and time again, until we begin to understand that scarcity doesn't mean God isn't blessing. We begin to learn to trust God's ability to see us through regardless of what the current circumstances may be. God is developing our character. We are learning to not panic. When trials come, rather than running from God, we run to Him. We don't deny God's trustworthiness but cling to it in times of adversity. We have gained the character of a believer. We know God is there, knows our need, cares about us, and won't abandon us.

And in that realization, we have taken hold of *hope*. Regardless of how desperate the situation seems, how empty the cupboards are, how low the checkbook balance is, how drained our energies have become, or how strained our relationships are, God is able to bring His provision—manna. He is able to provide what we need. He hasn't lost His focus on us. We choose to believe He cares and will come through. We have hope!

It all seems odd to the nonbeliever. My mom and dad married way too young. They had four children by the time they were twenty-three, and they had fallen away from God. They had separated five times but were now living together. Their lives were a royal mess without God, and they knew it.

On the morning of Sunday, February 21, 1971, Mom and Dad took us to church, and through God's grace Mom made the critical choice to believe. She asked Jesus into her heart. She told God she wanted Him more than anything else. Her heart recited Job 13:15 as a testimony of her faith: "Though he slay me, yet will I hope in him." As we headed home, she let Dad know she was determined to stay true to God no matter what. He wasn't happy. This was sure to mean problems.

When the time came to go to evening service, Mom begged Dad to go. He refused. He wasn't getting dragged into this one. Mom knew desperate times called for desperate measures. "That's fine. I'm going to leave the four boys with you, though, so I can enjoy the service." Needless to say, Dad was in church that night.

He fought the Holy Spirit throughout the entire sermon, giving every reason why he shouldn't give his heart to Christ. The altar call began, and my father was resisting the Holy Spirit's pull. He was on crutches at the time, and they were his last excuse. "Lord, I would have to get these crutches out and hobble all the way down to the altar." Little did he know, God had moved on the pastor's heart, and he was already standing beside Dad. "Kenny, don't you want to give your heart to Jesus tonight? Don't worry about the crutches. I'll help you down the aisle." Dad believed. He knelt at an altar of prayer and gave his life to Jesus. My mom and dad were truly restored as a household of faith that night as God began teaching them His ability to provide.

If faith were a fairytale, the next year would have been free of any trial. But faith in Jesus leads to a cross. Jesus was honest: "In this world you will have trouble" (John 16:33). Living on manna thrives on the promise that accompanies this brutal admission: "But take heart! I have overcome the world." Mom and Dad were going to learn the lesson of peace in the midst of trouble. During the year following their spiritual transformation, Dad lost his job and was in a car accident that could have taken his life. The well at their house dried up, and their furniture was repossessed.

It is at times like this that most of us cry out in accusation to God, "I thought You cared about me! I've chosen to follow You. Where are You?" But Mom and Dad were learning that God uses adversity to produce character. Dad got a better job, his life was spared from the drunk driver who hit him, and we moved to a better house. One day my mom was talking with her mother-in-law and she exclaimed, "This is so exciting! I just can't wait to see what God does next." My grandmother looked at her with astonishment and said, "Are you crazy?"

What appears as nonsense to those who don't believe God has their back makes perfect sense to those whose character has been transformed by adversity. The unbeliever says, "See! You are all alone!" The believer sees *hope* that is centered in God's caring presence in his or her life. The terrible circumstance may still cause your knees to shake. However, the emotions express themselves in anticipation instead of distrust. It isn't "*if* God comes through" but "*when* God comes through."

It's Time to Settle the Question

We must come to the place where we choose to believe God is here, and not just on a fairytale level. God is here and He knows our needs. More than that, He cares and doesn't take His attention off us.

When we really believe this, peace can dominate our attitude. Yes, when adversity hits, we will struggle to maintain that sense of being protected. Yes, we will call out to God with desperate persistence. But the heart of our cry will be based on the bedrock belief that God is present and cares. Anticipation, rather than accusation, will provide the basis for our emotional plea to God.

God wants to bless our lives with the daily miracles of His provision. Before we will be able to accept that kind of daily, absolute dependence on His ability to provide, we must make up our minds about what we really believe: "I believe my God is here. I believe He cares about me. I believe He never loses focus on my needs. I believe He can be trusted to meet my needs. I believe I can quit running after the blessings and can seek the Blessing Giver." Now we can choose to seek Him first and trust Him to provide what He knows we need—even if He provides it one day at a time. That kind of character produces a hope that cannot be shattered. "Give us today our daily bread"! We are living on manna!

3 THE QUESTION OF PROVISION
What Keeps Me Safe?

He is my stronghold, my refuge and my savior (2 Sam. 22:3).

The second question we each must answer if we are going to embody Jesus' call to live on manna, "Give us today our daily bread," is "What keeps me safe?" This is the question of provision. What sources of safety will we turn to when our spiritual journey gets tough?

When We Feel Abandoned . . .

I will never forget our joy when we found out Diana was pregnant with our first child. Everything changed. Suddenly all the things that were once important were now filtered through an unfathomable love for a child we'd never met.

Diana was four months along and showing. She was never more beautiful. Life was never richer. God's blessing could not be experienced with more depth and joy than through this miracle of life. I could never have imagined that this blessing would lead my wife and me to the most serious spiritual crisis of our lives. It was a crisis that would call into question whether we trusted God no matter what.

Diana and I grew up as church kids. We never really questioned whether God could be trusted. He was the hero of every Sunday School lesson. He was the God of the miraculous. In our naïveté, we just assumed God would continue to bless us in ways that would lead us along still waters. But now in the months to come we would have to decide whether He could be trusted even if His blessing led us through the valley of the shadow of death.

There was little we enjoyed more than placing our hands on Diana's stomach to feel the flutters of life growing inside her. But one morning everything changed, and Diana's cries signaled the beginning of our journey into the valley of shadows.

The early signs of a miscarriage are horrifying. That morning the frightening visit to the doctor ended with Diana being confined to bed for six weeks. Our daughter was still alive, but the joy of this reality could not penetrate our sense of extreme vulnerability. Our daughter's life was at risk.

Our absolute sense of God's trustworthiness was being challenged at its core. How could He let this happen? Surely He could be trusted to come through for us during this time. It was hard enough to comprehend that our Heavenly Protector was leading us through all of this, but the thought that He might have ignored our pleas was more than we could bear. We were fighting for our faith in God's ability to protect us. As shocked as we were at God's behavior, we had to try something to maintain our idealistic understanding of God's provision.

We pulled all the right levers on God's cosmic vending machine. We followed everything Scripture told us to do to get our Heavenly Protector to provide for us. We knew the "formula": "Is any one of you sick? He should call the elders of the church to pray over him and anoint him with oil in the name of the Lord. And the prayer offered in faith will make the sick person well; the Lord will raise him up" (James 5:14-15).

This was a *promise.* God could be trusted. He would keep our child safe. And so, we prayed, "God, You told us that if we ask anything in Your name, You will give it. Lord, this is not a selfish prayer. This prayer is for our child's life! We are living in faith. We are choosing to believe that You will heal."

"Good Christians" pray and believe—this was our driving hope. I was anointed at church for Diana. Our entire church family and friends across the country were all praying. It calmed our fears. God *had* to protect us now.

Diana was amazing. She never doubted God, not once. When I would begin to panic, I would look at her and ask her how she was doing. "I'm going to be fine, Kevin. We've prayed. They laid hands on you. God promised, and He will protect us."

We simply were not prepared to comprehend a God who protects us in ways we don't want. Our understanding of God's blessing would not allow for His will to be so against what we understood to be the only morally acceptable provision for our need. But God is God, and sometimes His provision simply isn't delivered according to our preferences.

We headed to the doctor for the ultrasound. We were so ready to praise God for His miraculous hand. All the preparations were done—the prayers, the anointing, the faith. This was God's opportunity to shine before these medical professionals. I played the scene over and over in my mind. We would shout for joy and tell the doctors about how God had done this. That's the way God works. He delivers the miracle in a way that allows us the opportunity to praise Him before the world. However, His answer on this day would leave me silent.

"There is no heartbeat. I'm sorry," were the doctor's words before he turned and left the room. Denial is an amazing thing. We heard the words, but it took some time to register that he had just pronounced our little girl's death. And so there we were in that cold room, grieving, angry, and very, very alone.

We could not sense God's presence in that moment. All we could feel was emotional torment, pain, and abandonment, none of which could be reconciled with our perfect picture of a God who protects.

Diana's parents had been on their way to our home in Lafayette, Indiana. They were originally coming to take care of Diana while I was busy at junior high camp, but now that was no longer necessary. At least they would be present while Diana underwent the concluding medical procedures.

Diana's night on the maternity ward was an emotional slap in the face. An incredible nurse made the pain more bearable. But here we were in the place where we should be celebrating life, and instead we were about to endure the final step in accepting death. How could we believe in a God who protects when the circumstances so clearly prove the opposite?

The next months would lead Diana and me down very different paths emotionally. Her disappointment in God's protection left her numb. She had emotionally given up on God. Yes, she believed He was there. But if He couldn't be trusted to protect her when she needed it most, then why even care? He was not her Protector. He was not anything to be trusted. He was nothing.

I was angry. I played the part of a loving husband and good pastor. However, I couldn't imagine how a God who is supposed to love us could be so evil as to play such a hideous joke. "Here is the prayer you pray. Trust Me. I'll come through for you!" Right! Been there, done that—never again. I couldn't escape the teachings of my youth. In my heart I knew God had to be there, but I just wasn't sure I wanted to worship Him anymore. He couldn't be trusted. He wasn't a protector but an insincere giant who barely paid attention to us. If He truly had our best interest at heart, if He truly could be trusted to protect us, He would have answered our prayers the way we knew He should have—the way He promised!

Provision Unseen

That summer, I was scheduled to help a good friend prepare his church for the prospect of hiring of a youth pastor. I was assigned to engender excitement in his leaders for this idea, while leading their group through a retreat. This was a one-weekend trip—nothing life-changing.

As I prepared to get in my car to head back to my hurting wife, my friend pulled me into his office and said, "I know you only came up here to get my people ready to start looking for a youth pastor. I know we can't pay you what you make right now. And I know you really don't want another youth pastor assignment. But I want you to start praying about becoming my associate."

"I appreciate your confidence," I told him, "but God would have to beat me over the head with a two-by-four to get me to take another position." I got in the car and God beat me all the way home. It made no sense. The church was smaller. The pay was less. There was no established youth ministry and nothing to build on. My wife was hurting. "Don't make a move within a year of a major tragedy" was the counseling advice I knew I would give to others. But God was bringing His provision, even when I couldn't see it.

The move to Fort Wayne came within a few months of the loss of our daughter. Diana was still emotionally dead. "I don't care what you do." That's how she prayed through on the move. If I had had two bits of sense, I would have known this is not what we "should" do. But even in the midst of my anger and her despair, God was leading us to manna.

It wasn't long before my new senior pastor took me to lunch. He was setting me up with an endless basket of tortilla chips. "How's Diana?" he asked. "She's doing fine. She'll be all right," I answered. His next words would prove to be the vehicle through which God's true provision for Diana would come. "No she's not, Kevin. She's dying inside and you can't see it." He handed me the name of a counselor and with the responsibility and concern of a true friend told me to make the appointment.

Over the next weeks God would use this counselor—a man we'd never met who lived in a place we never expected to be—to open our hearts to the idea that God can love and protect us, even in ways we cannot explain. Referencing Deut. 32:10, the counselor told us, "You are the very apple of God's eye. That means you are the center of His attention. He never loses focus on you and your needs." It took some time to understand. We had to take another look at our tragedy. Where we thought we had been abandoned, God had simply been providing in unseen ways.

Diana's mom and dad were on their way to our house the very week we lost the baby. Coincidence? Some might say so. I had to go to junior high camp. That's why they were coming. But we were learning to see the provision in the pain—the protection we could not have planned. The God who never loses His focus on our needs had provided a source of comfort for my wife I could never have provided. His timing was perfect. We were learning to recognize the manna in the desert.

The nurse who stayed with Diana through the night in the maternity ward was not supposed to be on that shift. Her attentiveness to Diana's needs made the horrific situation more tenable. The other nurses simply didn't know what to say to Diana. They came and left quietly, which only added to her pain. But God had sent this dear lady as an angel of mercy. He had protected Diana in the middle of the most difficult night of her life.

Even the counselor now leading us to healing was part of God's unseen provision. I wasn't planning to move to another associate pastor's position. I wasn't even sure I could stay in ministry. But God had moved us to Fort Wayne so He could lead us to this part of His provision.

Choosing to Believe God Keeps Us Safe

Because Diana and I experienced our grief differently, we also found faith in our Heavenly Protector differently. Diana had a very profound discussion with God. God did the talking: "Diana, I've let you be angry with Me for a long time now. That's

OK. But it's time to make a choice. You can go on being mad at Me if you want. But if you do that, I can't use you. I know I don't always do things the way you want. But you are going to have to make up your mind to trust Me. You are going to have to decide if you are going to follow Me because I always do what you want, or if you are going to follow Me because I am God." It was a pivotal decision. Diana made up her mind to trust the declaration of God: "You are the apple of My eye." She chose to trust God to protect her, to keep her safe, even when life is tough.

I regained my faith in God in a very different way. As much as I had heard Deut. 32:10 and was trying to believe God never loses focus on our needs, I was still having a difficult time understanding how God could have broken His promise to provide healing for my daughter.

It was Easter Sunday morning and the choir was singing their cantata. But I couldn't tell you anything about it, because I had spent the morning mentally sparring with God: "How can You explain why You didn't do what You promised? We prayed, we were anointed, we believed! But You didn't heal. You didn't keep Your promise." And then the muffled sounds of the choir grabbed my attention as they sang about the Resurrection. I don't remember the exact words, but the message was clear. God raised Jesus to life so that death cannot keep its hold on us. And then God spoke tender words of transformation to my heart.

"Kevin, I provided the answer to your daughter's death long before she would need it. I know you would have preferred to have seen your daughter grow up. But My Son provided for your need, and, Kevin, she is alive! And you will see her one day."

At that moment I had to make a choice. Would I accept God's provision on His terms? Would I choose to believe that He keeps me safe, even when He does it in ways that are unexpected and sometimes uninvited? Yes! I finally understood the words of Paul:

"Where, O death, is your victory? Where, O death, is your sting?" The sting of death is sin, and the power of sin is the law. But thanks be to God! He gives us the victory through our Lord Jesus Christ. Therefore, my dear brothers, stand firm. Let nothing move you. Always give yourselves fully to the work of the Lord, because you know that your labor in the Lord is not in vain. (1 Cor. 15:55-58)

God can be trusted to protect us. He has provided the ultimate protection—resurrection. Even the finality of my daughter's death had been undone. The pain was temporary. God wasn't conquered. No, I didn't like His timing. Yes, I wish I could experience all of God's blessings right here and now. But I must choose to believe I am safe, not only when God's provision is immediate, but also when it is unseen.

Ultimately, there is no hardship, no scarcity, no pain that can undo the provision given through the Resurrection. I can endure whatever trial today brings because I trust the Blessing Giver. He has protected me, and I choose to believe He keeps me safe.

It really doesn't matter what the circumstances are that call us to question God's ability to keep us safe. If we are going to enjoy God's provision no matter what form or timing He uses, we will have to trust that He is protecting us. We are the apple of His eye.

One God—One Source of Safety

When we accept God to be the one trusted source of safety in our lives, we can walk into tomorrow without needing to know what tomorrow holds. We know that the One who has asked us to take this step of faith is the One who keeps us safe, so we don't need to know how He is going to handle every detail of the journey. Until we clearly answer the question of provision—"What keeps me safe?"—we will turn to every source of safety but God. And in so doing, we will become idolaters. Gutsy faith, the kind that can sleep at night knowing manna is coming in the morning, will only develop when we refuse to worship other gods—other sources of safety.

In Exod. 24, Moses left the children of Israel to go up to the mountain to meet God. In Exod. 32, after Moses' prolonged absence, the Israelites panicked. Their tangible evidence of God's protection (Moses) was gone. And so they called on Aaron to make "gods" who would protect them. Aaron instructed them to bring their earrings, and he threw them into the fire. They crafted a golden calf and began to worship it. It sounds ludicrous, but it reflects our very first instinct.

When things get complicated, we want tangible sources of safety. We want a bank account that is large enough to handle the financial crisis. We want a spouse who is capable enough to lead us through the difficult days. We want a job that will give us meaning. We want toys that will validate our success. The list is endless. Just like the Israelites who faced a day when they felt alone, we turn to everything but God to give us a sense that everything is going to be OK.

Don't Worship the Blessings

The children of Israel made a horrible declaration in Exod. 32:4. After seeing the hand of God bring them out of Egypt, care for their needs, and defeat their enemy, they looked at the sources of safety they had created for themselves—the golden calf—and said, "These are your gods, O Israel, who brought you up out of Egypt."

This is our great temptation—to take the blessings of God

and worship them as gods—sources of safety. Anything in our lives that becomes a replacement in our hearts for God as our one source of safety has become a "god" to us. We receive the blessing, the manna, and because we can see it, touch it, smell it, and so on, we choose to trust the blessing for our safety. We are low on money, so we pray and ask God to help. He sends the manna we requested. Now we are faced with the temptation to trust the money more than the God who sent it. We are tempted to hoard it, protect it, and value it above all other things. It doesn't matter what our scarcity is—money, time, energy, freedom, security, and so on—we are always tempted to trust it for our safety.

Refuse to Trust Other Sources of Safety

We are each tempted by different sources of safety. They are as different as our personalities. While we will discuss a few of the more common areas of temptation, we must understand that anything in our lives that we run to for protection has become a "god" in our lives. We must be very careful to enjoy the blessings, to utilize the resources at our disposal, but at all times maintain a proper relationship between ourselves, God, and the resources. Not one of the areas of life we will discuss, except for addictions, is in and of itself bad. However, when we shift from God to these things for our sense of what keeps us safe, we have lost a critical balance and need to adjust our hearts accordingly.

Finances

Money is the only thing in all of Scripture that Jesus ever referred to as being in absolute competition for our love for God (Matt. 6:24). Every one of us is tempted to trust finances more than God for our safety. Whether the issue is committing God's tithe to Him on a consistent basis, being willing to sacrifice to meet the needs of friends and family, or simply continuing in God's will when it costs us financially, we all suffer under the false belief that we are safe when we have enough money.

Don't get me wrong. We all tend to panic when funds are tight. You can expect your emotions to pull you hard during those times. The question here is whether our obedience is dependent on having enough money.

A friend of mine spent several years in full-time evangelism. His fall, winter, and spring were always spent holding revival services in churches across the country. However, summer for an evangelist, especially a young evangelist, can be a time when speaking engagements, and thus money, are in short supply.

Scott was experiencing one of those summers. He was working for a landscape company to get by. However, the cupboards were almost bare and he was out of money. Things were so bad that Scott didn't even have a lunch to take to work. Many of us would have spent the day screaming accusations at God: "How can You abandon me when I have given up so much for You?" Scott would have been more than justified to reject his call, find a good-paying job, and take care of his family. But instead, Scott spent the day on his lawnmower pouring out his soul to God.

He was mowing the lawn at the local gas station, still praying for God's intervention when manna appeared on the ground— literally on the ground. Scott looked down onto the grass to find a twenty-dollar bill. He picked up the money and started praising God! A few feet further he found another twenty-dollar bill. Scott had responded to his scarcity properly: "God, You are my only source of protection. If You don't provide, I'm not going to eat!" God protects in unexpected ways, just in time, with just enough. He provides manna. The experience served to strengthen Scott's faith in the God who protects.

Relationships

For some, relationships become the "gods" who are sure to deliver them out of despair. Janette° had grown more spiritually in the last few years than any time I had known her. She was growing closer to God and was taking on more responsibility in the church. But she was in her mid-twenties and still single. It was really beginning to worry her—surely God did not intend for her to be alone.

When the relationship began, her attendance at church became more and more sporadic. My honesty had to be hard to take when I said to her, "You want to be married so much that you aren't waiting on God's timing." Her boyfriend didn't value God and really wanted nothing to do with church. It wasn't long before her desire for God was replaced with a desire for this young man, and she completely abandoned God.

The relationship didn't last. Nothing born out of abandonment to God's provision does. The days to come were full of pain and embarrassment. Janette came back to God and now testifies to His provision, even as she waits on God's "Mr. Right."

This dependency on relationships over God is also expressed in marriage. Things get rough and we emotionally turn to our spouse with the expectation that he or she should keep us safe. "You aren't earning enough money!" "Why don't you do more to make me feel safe?" "If you really loved me, you wouldn't ask me to go through this." Shame and blame become powerful weapons of manipulation as we try to get the ones we love to behave in ways we think will solve our problems. In facing the normal adversities of life we have shifted the responsibility to keep us safe. No longer do we rely on God but on our loved ones.

°Fictitious name representing a composite of several individuals known by author throughout twenty years of ministry.

Possessions/Accumulation

While relationships might be the "god" of choice for some, "stuff" is the god that tempts others: "I know I am safe when I have the perfect house, a great car, the latest toys, and so on. It doesn't matter that I violate stewardship principles to get these things. It doesn't matter if the Holy Spirit is telling me to wait. I *need* this or that and I will have it!" Credit cards are maxed out before you know it. The variable rate on the mortgage has risen so much that the monthly payment is no longer possible. The latest toys are unfashionable long before they've been paid off. Rather than learning contentment in whatever abundance God has provided, we have once again behaved like "pagans" and have run after other sources of safety.

Personal Ability

This is one of the more clandestine "sources of safety." It masquerades as "maturity." From an early age we are taught that being mature is the ability to stand on our own two feet. And this is partly correct. We need to take personal responsibility for our behavior, our goals, our decisions, and so on. But there is a difference between taking responsibility for what is within our control, and buying into the idea that we are only safe when we are "in control."

When we believe we are safe only when we are in control of everything and everyone around us, we cannot be used by God. Many times God asks us to walk into territory where only He can control the circumstances. Like crossing the Red Sea, or walking around the walls of Jericho, there are times when God is going to have to do something miraculous that you and I cannot do if we are going to make it. The powerful thing is that those times become the hallmark moments of our faith development. Those are the times we tell our children and grandchildren about. If we trust our personal ability so much that we are unwilling to risk following God into times when our ability isn't enough, we will miss much of the great adventure God has designed.

I am not saying we should become so contrite that we ignore all the gifts with which God has endowed us. We need to have a "sober" understanding of how God has gifted us and use those gifts as a great source of blessing (Rom. 12:3). We are in fact expressing faith in God's ability to enable us. That is healthy and right.

However, living on manna means we accept that God will lead us into territory where the giants are bigger than us. But we will make a choice to see the milk and honey that flows in the land God has determined to deliver into our hands. We will choose our obedience on the basis of God's ability rather than ours. Our sense of safety won't be limited by our ability but determined by God's ability. Where others will walk away from God's plan because they are convinced of their inability, we will face danger with an absolute confidence in God's call.

Stability

For many, stability is sought after first and foremost when the tough times hit. I know I am safe because I am still liked. I am getting along with everyone, so it is OK. I don't want to walk into this day of confrontation. I am not safe unless everything in life is just right.

The danger in turning to stability as our source of safety rather than God is that life is rarely stable when we are walking with the Man who disrupted the system so much that they crucified Him for it. It is difficult to imagine that the spiritual journey Jesus defined as "taking up your cross and following me" will enjoy consistent stability. Following Jesus requires a love for the thrill of riding proverbial roller coasters.

And yet, many of us are convinced that the only time God

is truly watching out for us is when all of life is calm. I would suggest that we must reject this idea in hand. Jesus was clear: "Remember the words I spoke to you: 'No servant is greater than his master.' If they persecuted me, they will persecute you also. If they obeyed my teaching, they will obey yours also. They will treat you this way because of my name, for they do not know the One who sent me" (John 15:20-21).

Now, I am not suggesting that a sign of a good Christian is that he or she leaves a mess in his or her wake. That is not what Jesus is getting at. In fact, we are warned against such behavior (see 1 Pet. 2:12). However, Jesus is giving us a very realistic picture of how to understand God's protection. He will not protect us from persecution by a world that disdains the gospel of Jesus Christ.

You can expect people to get angry when you stand up for what is right. You can expect your children to fight you over the rules. You can expect coworkers to challenge your commitment to ethics that seem too rigid. When such realities cause us to reject God or to lessen our obedience to Him, we have chosen stability as our source of safety.

Stability in life has nothing to do with God's protection. Like Shadrach, Meshach, and Abednego, we understand that sometimes God meets us in the fire (see Dan. 3). When we travel with Jesus, we must choose to acknowledge that God's provision and protection are often found in the middle of the storm. We do not respond like the disciples who awakened Jesus to inform Him that they were going to die (see Matt. 8:25); we cry out to Jesus because we know He controls the storm.

Addictions

What do addictions have to do with sources of safety? We have to understand that many addictions are simply a medicine we use to comfort our pain. For some, the medicine is eating.

For others, spending is our natural response to painful circum-stances. Whether the addiction is heroine, Twinkies, Visa, por-nography, or one of thousands of others, we are turning to that thing as a source of comfort to deal with our pain.

When I choose to use one of these things as a medicine for pain, I am turning to it as a source of safety. I am making a choice to turn to something other than God to make me feel better in the middle of a very difficult situation. Although the intent and scope of this book does not include laying out a path to healing from all addictions, we must come to grips with an important reality: When we allow an addiction to become our source of safety, we are cheating ourselves of the miracle that comes from allowing the hand of God to deliver peace to our situation. "I am convinced I need this or that to make it through this ordeal. And so, it has become a 'god' to me." As Jesus did when He was tempted in the desert, we have got to decide what we need to survive.

What Did Jesus Trust?

Jesus understood what was at stake in the temptations re-corded in Matt. 4. His ministry wouldn't begin until some very crucial issues were settled. Jesus had just been baptized. The Holy Spirit inaugurated His ministry as the Messiah. But before His ministry could begin, Jesus would spend 40 days fasting and praying in the desert. This time of spiritual preparation would conclude with a series of fundamental temptations. The first of those temptations deals with the very heart of this chapter: "What keeps me safe?"

The temptation comes when Jesus is at the bottom of His barrel physically. He has a deep need for physical nourishment. But this time in the desert isn't about meeting His physical needs. It is about preparing His spirit for the journey to which God had called Him. And when His need is at its most demanding, the question of provision comes: "The tempter came to him and said, 'If you are the Son of God, tell these stones to become bread.' Jesus answered, 'It is written: "Man does not live on bread alone, but on every word that comes from the mouth of God""" (Matt. 4:3-4).

Here Jesus had to decide what He trusted to keep Him safe. "Will I survive because I have what I need physically? Do I need to have enough for tomorrow to trust God with today? What is it that keeps Me safe?"

Jesus' answer helps us understand the source of our safety. He declared that He was alive because of "every word that comes from the mouth of God" (v. 4). Thus, we live because of God's words—His declaration. He tells us to follow; it is safe to follow. He tells us He will never leave us or forsake us; it is safe to trust Him. Our safety isn't determined by how much bread we have, how much food is in the cupboard, or how much money is in the checkbook. Our safety is anchored in God's declaration in our lives. Our safety rests in one source of protection, and only one—God. What He says goes. If a difficult situation comes to us, God has it under control. It doesn't matter how hard it is for us to understand. It doesn't matter whether or not we feel we can handle it. God is with us, so we are OK. We are safe because of His declaration.

Safety Through Obedience to God's Call

Our survival is dependent on our obedience, not our abundance. This is the pattern of resurrection Paul teaches us in Phil. 2:8-9:

And being found in appearance as a man,
he humbled himself
and became obedient to death—
even death on a cross!

Therefore God exalted him to the highest place
and gave him the name that is above every name.

God's protection of Jesus, His resurrection, was complete because Jesus was obedient to God's plan all the way to death. If we are obedient to God, we can trust Him to protect us, even when it appears that all is lost. Even death cannot claim final victory over the person who places God as his or her one trusted source of protection.

Jesus was able to stay obedient to God's plan, even as He faced the brutality of the Cross, because He had settled the question of what kept Him safe long before. When Jesus chose to trust God's declaration as His source of safety over all other provisions, He was ready to follow God's plan to its end. It didn't matter that the end would cost Jesus His life. Even His life would not be a litmus test for safety. God's declaration, His will, was the only standard for measuring safety. So we are safe when we are obedient to God.

Jesus Is Our Manna

So once we decide what we truly need to be safe, God will be able to use us to do His will. And what do we need beyond anything else? Jesus tells us in John 6 that God has given us exactly what we need to be safe. He has provided the ultimate manna from heaven. It is Jesus himself. But even though God has provided us with exactly what we need in Jesus, we are still tempted to seek physical abundance when we should be seeking *Him.*

As John 6 recounts, Jesus miraculously served dinner to 5,000 people. Using five small loaves and a couple fish, Jesus provided an abundance these people would not soon forget. He was their meal ticket, and they weren't about to lose that! So they went looking for Him. When they found Him, Jesus called their motivation into question. His words challenge our own attitudes today. Again, what is it that keeps us safe? Are we seeking provision or the One who provides?

Jesus answered, "I tell you the truth, you are looking for me, not because you saw miraculous signs but because you ate the loaves and had your fill. Do not work for food that spoils, but for food that endures to eternal life, which the Son of Man will give you. On him God the Father has placed his seal of approval."

Then they asked him, "What must we do to do the works God requires?"

Jesus answered, "The work of God is this: to believe in the one he has sent."

So they asked him, "What miraculous sign then will you give that we may see it and believe you? What will you do? Our forefathers ate the manna in the desert; as it is written: 'He gave them bread from heaven to eat.'"

Jesus said to them, "I tell you the truth, it is not Moses who has given you the bread from heaven, but it is my Father who gives you the true bread from heaven. For the bread of God is he who comes down from heaven and gives life to the world."

"Sir," they said, "from now on give us this bread."

Then Jesus declared, "I am the bread of life. He who comes to me will never go hungry, and he who believes in me will never be thirsty." (John 6:26-35)

These people weren't seeking to live under the miraculous hand of God. They had one concern—where will we get a meal today? They were living under the frightening perspective of self-protection. They were so overwhelmed with creating their own way of escape that they couldn't see that God had provided a source of provision that couldn't be exhausted. They were standing in front of the Manna of heaven and were asking for bread!

We do the same thing. God wants to teach us that His presence is what provides safety, not our resources. He has promised to bless us as we accept Jesus as our only trusted resource. But we still shout and scream, "God, we are all alone here! We are going to die!" Living on manna means we have to accept that in Jesus, God has provided everything we need. We are not safe because we have enough money, but because God owns everything. We are not safe because we have a house, but because God is the Creator of the universe. We are not safe because any of these other "sources of safety" are with us, but because Jesus, the Manna from heaven, lives in us. He has promised never to abandon us.

And so we must choose to place our trust in Jesus. That is, we must refuse to seek any other blessing as the thing that keeps us safe. We must have no other god before Him. We must worship—place our sense of safety—in Christ and Christ alone. He is the food that endures to eternal life.

The people in John 6 asked an important question, "What must we do to do the works God requires?" Jesus called them to first answer the question of belief: "The work of God is this: to believe in the one he has sent." But this wasn't enough. The crowd wanted another miracle, and so they pushed Jesus: "Give us a sign so we can believe in you" (author's paraphrase). They were being quite honest. "We aren't willing to just believe. We have to *see;* then we will believe. So prove yourself first."

If we weren't so much like these people, we might say, "How foolish!" But to be honest, we each must admit we have uttered similar words to God many times over: "God, I want to believe, but I need another sign." Yet, Jesus drives home the heart of the issue: "I am the Miracle!" He reminds them of the manna that God miraculously provided for the children of Israel. It was a daily reminder of God's provision and protection. Jesus now stands as the final authentication of God's trustworthiness. He is our manna. He has our back! We are safe!

When we believe in Jesus, we accept the reality that God has provided protection for us that other sources of safety simply cannot provide. He is calling us to stop needing to see the miracle before we are able to believe God has provided it. We see Jesus and we believe. So we trust God. If He provided this great salvation while we were His enemies, we can be sure He will protect us through whatever trials may come now that we are His children. Jesus is God's promise—"I've got your back!"

The beauty of this manna is that it is never-ending. "He who comes to me will never go hungry, and he who believes in me will never be thirsty." We may not like it that God's provision is poured out on us one day at a time. We might prefer that He make a delivery at least a week or two in advance. However, we choose to believe that His storehouse cannot be depleted. Jesus is our evidence of God's capacity to meet our needs. God is our endless supply of safety. We are OK because He is present. We are safe, not because of the trustworthiness of any other source of safety, but because the Blessing Giver has an endless supply of all we need.

4 THE QUESTION OF VALUES

Is Enough for Today Enough for Me?

But seek first his kingdom and his righteousness, and all these things will be given to you as well. Therefore do not worry about tomorrow, for tomorrow will worry about itself. Each day has enough trouble of its own (Matt. 6:33-34).

Thorny Soil

The third question we must answer if we are to adopt Jesus' call to live on manna is the question of values. Jesus is calling each of us to a value system where daily provision is enough for obedience. "Is enough for today enough for me?" It is a question we must be able to answer yes to if we are going to experience the transformational power of God's Word in our lives. It isn't easy. However, Jesus identified this question as crucial for God's Word to take hold and produce fruit in our lives.

A farmer went out to sow his seed. As he was scattering the seed, some fell along the path, and the birds came and ate it up. Some fell on rocky places, where it did not have much soil. It sprang up quickly, because the soil was shallow. But when the sun came up, the plants were scorched, and they withered because they had no root. Other seed fell among thorns, which grew up and choked the plants. Still other seed fell on good soil, where it produced a crop—a hundred, sixty or thirty times what was sown. He who has ears, let him hear. . . . The one who received the seed that fell among the thorns is the man who hears the word, but the worries of this life and the deceitfulness of wealth choke it, making it unfruitful. (Matt. 13:3-9, 22)

The call to live on daily bread means we have to really evaluate what we value most. We must evaluate the level to which materialism is choking our ability to have a vital relationship with God. We live in a world that values the accumulation of "stuff" above all else. And Jesus calls us to develop a heart that only needs what we "need." Will we allow ourselves to become unshackled to our thirst for more and more? It isn't that having things is wrong. However, we must honestly evaluate whether or not we have allowed our sense of purpose to be determined by this ability to gather stuff.

Is "Enough for Today" Enough for Me?

Jesus is clear that wealth is not the thing that causes God's Word to be "choked" out of our lives. It is the "deceit of wealth" along with the worries of this life that choke God's Word and keep it from being fruitful in us—from transforming us. The deceit of wealth can be understood as many things, but fundamentally the deceitfulness of wealth is the lie that the accumulation of wealth and a life of "consumption" should be our highest value. It leads us to believe that money keeps us safe, makes us happy, and is worth fighting for our entire lives. That lie causes us to lose our faith in God's place as our one trusted source of provision. Instead of being thirsty for God, we become thirsty for "stuff." God's Word has no place to take hold and call us to daily dependence.

Jesus calls us to a completely different value system. His value system says that life is about an intimate relationship with the Father that is open to His transformational intrusion in our lives. This value system isn't dependent on abundance to know when life is right.

For many of us, this goes directly against the value system we have embraced. Our entire lives are focused on the accumulation and consumption of material blessings. So when Jesus calls us to take up the value system of daily bread, we are confronted with something that is frightening. Like the rich young ruler in Matthew, we each must answer this fundamental question of values, "Is enough for today enough for me?" Can we follow Jesus if it means abandoning a value system committed to accumulation?

Let's listen as Jesus confronts the rich young ruler and instructs His disciples. They are each grappling with the question of values.

Jesus looked at him and loved him. "One thing you lack," he said. "Go, sell everything you have and give to the poor, and you will have treasure in heaven. Then come, follow me."

At this the man's face fell. He went away sad, because he had great wealth.

Jesus looked around and said to his disciples, "How hard it is for the rich to enter the kingdom of God!"

The disciples were amazed at his words. But Jesus said again, "Children, how hard it is to enter the kingdom of God! It is easier for a camel to go through the eye of a needle than for a rich man to enter the kingdom of God."

The disciples were even more amazed, and said to each other, "Who then can be saved?"

Jesus looked at them and said, "With man this is impossible, but not with God; all things are possible with God."

Peter said to him, "We have left everything to follow you!"

"I tell you the truth," Jesus replied, "no one who has left home or brothers or sisters or mother or father or children or fields for me and the gospel will fail to receive a hundred times as much in this present age (homes, brothers, sisters, mothers, children and fields—and with them, persecutions) and in the age to come, eternal life. But many who are first will be last, and the last first." (Mark 10:21-31)

The rich young ruler couldn't give up his trust in his material possessions. Jesus challenged his value system, and he wasn't prepared to abandon it. His obedience to the "rules" was perfect. He was a good Jewish man who followed the Law. But it wasn't enough. He didn't understand where true provision comes from. He had embraced a value system where his material possessions were more important than following Jesus. He could only follow up to a point—the point of sacrifice. His worship of material blessings was the true value system he used to make his decision.

While I disagree with those who say this scripture is a call for all believers to live in poverty, I do believe this passage is a universal call to reject the value system that worships "stuff" over the Creator. Jesus isn't saying everyone must sell his or her possessions in order to follow Him. He is calling us to abandon a value system that believes we must live in abundance to remain obedient to God's call.

The rich young ruler couldn't abandon his commitment to "stuff" in order to follow Jesus. On the other hand, the disciples declared, "We have left everything to follow you." This powerful comparison of two value systems becomes the platform for Jesus to remind us of God's economy. He does bless us and provide for us. But that blessing is reserved for those who have abandoned their worship of "stuff."

As Jesus says, those who give up their "brothers . . . sisters . . . fields," and so on, as objects of worship will receive so much more and eternal life too. This is the promise of provision. It isn't based on our ability to produce wealth for ourselves. The promise of provision is based on God's ability to bless. We can walk away from our thirst for material blessings, because we know God wants to bless us abundantly. It is safe to shift our thirst for "stuff" to a thirst for God. When we do that, God provides more than we will ever be able to provide for ourselves.

This isn't the "prosperity" doctrine so popular in many circles of Christianity today. Jesus doesn't promise we will receive the full storehouse at one time but that all of God's resources will be put at our disposal both now and in eternity. God blesses us abundantly. But He requires us to trust Him for the timing and amount of the provision. Moreover, Jesus reminds us the blessing is often accompanied by pain (persecution).

So if today we are living in scarcity, it doesn't mean God is not blessing or that our faith is somehow lacking. Whatever God provides for today, we must consider it enough for us to remain obedient. If we do not, then like the rich young ruler we will turn away. When enough for today is enough for us, then we step into days of incredible potential. God is now able to take us places where we would never have followed before. In those great adventures of faith, we are able to experience the miraculous provision of God.

Accumulation or Blessing?

I have experienced this call to follow, even when it meant walking away from abundance, in very real and frightening ways. I had pastored fourteen years and was finishing a master's in business administration when God called me to a journey into the unknown. After much prayer, I stepped out of full-time pastoral ministry to begin a ministry of finance. Through a series of miracles God had revealed His will, which led me of all places to a secular brokerage firm. "What am I doing here, God?" was often how my morning prayers began in the early days of that journey. "I am a pastor! I am about helping the church. Why am I in this cubicle?" But the Lord kept affirming, "Just learn all you can. I know what I am doing. Trust Me."

So I studied and learned all I could. It didn't take long before I realized that this work wasn't so bad. My income more than doubled the first year. It took awhile for me to be able to say, "I am a financial adviser." But before long, I realized people showed a great deal more respect when I uttered those words. More respect, more money—this obedience to God thing was working out just fine.

I tried to ignore the Spirit's warning: "Don't get too comfortable, Kevin. This isn't the end of the journey. I didn't bring you here to get rich." I reasoned that the still, small voice was just my "pastor's lifestyle" refusing to believe I was finally financially stable. I wanted to believe my obedience to God's call had resulted in a level of financial blessing I would have missed if I had refused to step out in faith. I would later realize that God's blessing had little to do with the financial provision I was currently experiencing. The blessing He was bringing was the opportunity to help others. That blessing would come because of these days invested in Pharaoh's court.

Three years later, God made good on His warning and asked me to step away from this financial security. It was time to take another risk of obedience. My work with churches in planned giving and financial consulting was blossoming. Eventually I had to choose between meeting the expectations of my employer and continuing my work with the churches. Was my life going to be about the material blessings of my "position" or the spiritual blessings of obedience to God's plan?

I knew what God wanted. But it was going to cost me dearly. I made the very difficult choice to establish the "endowments and stewardship" division at the Segue Foundation. Doing this meant leaving thousands of dollars of unrealized stock options and taking a 50 percent pay cut. I am not saying I enjoyed it. It was painful. There were many times when I shouted at God, "I have done what You asked me to do. I could use a little help here!"

It was in those days that I began to come to grips with God's call to live on manna. I didn't have the huge check coming every month. I didn't have a huge retirement plan or a great health care plan. But I did have God, and He came through every time, without exception. It didn't take long for me to realize what the true blessing of obedience was, and it wasn't "stuff."

In the first year at Segue, we began work with several denominations in the development of planned giving strategies. We helped many churches step into the next phase of their vision. My work with local churches expanded to statewide organizations. I was even invited to present a seminar on how to teach people to tithe to all the Indiana pastors of a large denomination! I remember thinking, *Who am I that I get to do this?* But God said, "You were obedient, and I am blessing."

While the financial adjustments were difficult and painful, the blessing of being used by God in these ways would never have been possible if I had refused to live on "daily provision." Yes, I could have chosen the safe route. I could have even justified it: "This is what is best for my family. My first responsibility is to them." But if I had done that, I would have missed all that God had in store. I would have chosen a value system that limits God's ability to take us into His blessing.

It isn't that God is calling us to poverty. There is nothing wrong with the material blessings He provides. However, we must refuse to place the accumulation of stuff as the value system through which we decide how far we will follow God. In Matt. 8 the teacher of the Law tells Jesus he will follow wherever Jesus goes. Jesus reminds the man that this journey will be difficult and provides no assurance of material abundance: "Then a teacher of the law came to him and said, 'Teacher, I will follow you wherever you go.' Jesus replied, 'Foxes have holes and birds of the air have nests, but the Son of Man has no place to lay his head'" (Matt. 8:19-20).

This is not saying we must live a life of poverty. However, it is a call to deal with our value system. Jesus doesn't promise material prosperity. He constantly calls us to keep our focus on the things of heaven. And when we do that, we will experience blessings that we could never find when our obedience is limited by our demand for a certain level of abundance.

Reject the Deceitfulness of Wealth

This need for accumulation and consumption is at the heart of the deceitfulness of wealth that Jesus said "chokes" the Word's ability to be fruitful in us. God, not wealth, is our blessing. We must reject the deceitfulness of wealth. Life is not about acquiring more stuff.

In Luke 15 Jesus tells the story of a young man who decided it was time for him to "live it up." He took his inheritance and headed out to live a life of accumulation and consumption. He had been living under the provision of his father. In his father's house he had everything he needed. But the heart controlled by the values of consumption and accumulation aren't satisfied with provision. He wanted to own the provision.

It didn't take long before the young man had squandered his wealth. He experienced the full impact of his thirst for more— he lost everything. He was so destitute that he was even envious of the food the pigs ate. It was at this moment, when he came to grips with his own inability to provide for his needs, that he came to his senses. His thirst for wealth led him to a sinful separation from the father. His life had been marked by full provision but was now a picture of utter destitution. It was time to set things right. He returned home and experienced the grace-filled embrace of his father.

There is much to learn from the attitude of this "prodigal son." His thirst for wealth led him away from the provision of the Father and ended with his utter destitution. He had enough provision for every day. But because he wasn't the owner, it wasn't enough. He left the home to fulfill his thirst for accumulation and consumption. He found that his ability to provide safety and sustenance for himself paled in comparison to the "sure" daily provision in his father's house. His thirst for consumption led him into a life of sin—a life that abandoned a proper relationship to the father. His salvation was to remember that his father was a trusted source of provision. This is the greatest lesson the prodigal teaches us. It is never too late to turn away from this messed-up value system and return to a life of blessing through provision.

A thirst for accumulation and consumption leads us away from the true source of provision—our Heavenly Father. However, like the prodigal, we never get so far away from God's design for our lives that we can't decide to turn around and go home.

This is one of the most difficult spiritual victories we will pursue. We must come to grips with the reality that God provides for us far better than we ever could. That is scary. God rarely gives us everything we need up front. He delivers it one piece at a time, just in time, and just enough for today. The spiritual victory is found in learning to remain obedient to God whether He pours out material abundance or chooses to provide for us one day at a time. Our provision is to be found in God's trustworthiness, not our abundance.

My colleague at Segue Foundation, Darrell Poeppelmeyer, loves to illustrate this reality with pie. He'll place in front of you an entire pie and a plate with one piece and then say, "You can have whichever one you want. You choose." It doesn't take too much intelligence to realize the entire pie is a better deal.

"Give me the whole thing!" you respond.

"OK," he chuckles, "but don't you want to know the rules?"

"What do you mean?"

"If you take the whole pie, that's all you get. But if you trust me to do what I promise, when you're done with the one piece, I will give you another one. In fact, I'll keep giving you another piece as long as you ask me. If you take the whole pie up front, you'll know exactly what you'll get. But if you trust me, you'll never run out."

As goofy as his illustration is, it drives home the picture of God's economy. When we value accumulation, we end up losing. When life is about consumption, we starve. However, when we trust God to provide, we always end up with more blessings than we could have provided for ourselves. Jesus puts it straight to us: "If anyone would come after me, he must deny himself and take up his cross and follow me. For whoever wants to save his life will lose it, but whoever loses his life for me will find it" (Matt. 16:24-25).

Our Highest Value—a Relationship with God

True followers value the relationship with the Father over the material blessings He provides. When the prodigal son returned home, the older brother responded to the Father's blessing with anger. Their interaction teaches us something about how God wants us to understand His blessing and our attitude:

The older brother became angry and refused to go in. So his father went out and pleaded with him. But he answered his father, "Look! All these years I've been slaving for you and never disobeyed your orders. Yet you never gave me even a young goat so I could celebrate with my friends. But when this son of yours who has squandered your property with prostitutes comes home, you kill the fattened calf for him!"

"My son," the father said, "you are always with me, and everything I have is yours." (Luke 15:28-31)

The true blessing of the older son was that he had always had the presence of the Father. The older brother wanted to argue that the Father had been unfair with his distribution of material blessings. But the Father reminds the son that regardless of how much "stuff" the older son might carry in his hand, he has the entire storehouse of the father at his disposal. The true blessing isn't how much abundance we carry in hand. Our blessing is God's presence with us, and His resources are aimed at our protection and provision.

We must embrace this value system. We are blessed! We may or may not have everything others have. It doesn't really matter. We have God, and He owns everything. We don't have to carry around His provision to know it is at our disposal when God knows we need it. This value system says, "Enough for today is enough for me because I know God has enough forever! Even if He delivers my provision one day at a time, I have enough faith in His love for me to follow Him."

Redirect My Thirst

As mentioned earlier, adopting this value system of living on manna doesn't mean we have to live in poverty. It does mean we must replace our thirst for more and more stuff with a thirst for more and more of God. We must refuse to limit our obedience by how many material blessings we get to take with us on the journey. Thus we will have to reject this culture's value system, which evaluates success according to our ability to acquire more than we need. That doesn't mean we shouldn't prepare for retirement or our children's college needs. It doesn't mean that enjoying life and creating memories is against God's design.

However, it does mean we need to answer the question of when enough is enough. It does mean we must determine how God would have us use our blessings to honor His will in our lives. It does mean we must thrive in the reality that God often delivers just enough blessing just in time. It does mean we must accept that God is the owner of all things and that we are only the managers of His possessions. It does mean we are just as blessed when He trusts us with a little as we are when He trusts us with much. That is because *He* is our blessing, not the "stuff." We are to hunger and thirst for righteousness, not accumulation. We are to seek *Him,* not His possessions, with our whole heart.

Enjoy the Blessing—Resist Arrogance

When Jesus was tempted by the devil just after His baptism, He resisted the temptation to turn the stones to bread by quoting Deut. 8:3. Listen to the quote in the context of the surrounding verses.

Be careful to follow every command I am giving you today, so that you may live and increase and may enter and possess the land that the LORD promised on oath to your forefathers. Remember how the LORD your God led you all the way in the desert these forty years, to humble you and to test you in order to know what was in your heart, whether or not you would keep his commands. He humbled you, causing you to hunger and then feeding you with manna, which neither you nor your fathers had known, to teach you that *man does not live on bread alone but on every word that comes from the mouth of the LORD.* Your clothes did not wear out and your feet did not swell during these forty years. Know then in your heart that as a man disciplines his son, so the LORD your God disciplines you. (Vv. 1-5, emphasis added)

As mentioned in chapter 3, Jesus had to make up His mind about His value system in the same way you and I do. We have to decide whether our lives are about accumulation or provision. Like Jesus, we must acknowledge that sometimes God leads us into the desert to experience a scarcity of resources. He does this to discipline us and to refine our hearts. We learn obedience in these difficult circumstances. We learn that God is able to stretch our resources farther than we could ever imagine. The God who fed thousands with a few loaves of bread and fish, and kept the children of Israel's clothes from wearing out for forty years, can handle our limited abilities, low cash flow, lack of time, and so on. When we can remain obedient when life is tough, we are becoming powerful tools in God's economy.

In the verses that follow, God gives a warning to the children of Israel that we must hear. We must resist arrogance while we enjoy the blessings:

> When you have eaten and are satisfied, praise the LORD your God for the good land he has given you. Be careful that you do not forget the LORD your God, failing to observe his commands, his laws and his decrees that I am giving you this day. Otherwise, when you eat and are satisfied, when you build fine houses and settle down, and when your herds and flocks grow large and your silver and gold increase and all you have is multiplied, then your heart will become proud and you will forget the LORD your God, who brought you out of Egypt, out of the land of slavery. (Deut. 8:10-14)

God provides the accumulation of material blessings. And at the same time, He warns us against the danger of receiving such blessings and then forgetting about Him. We could become filled with pride and forget that He is the source of our blessings. We may be tempted to take the credit for the blessings and in our arrogance lose our proper relationship to God: "You may say to yourself, 'My power and the strength of my hands have produced this wealth for me.' But remember the LORD your God, for it is he who gives you the ability to produce wealth, and so confirms his covenant, which he swore to your forefathers, as it is today" (vv. 17-18).

There is nothing wrong with wealth. In fact, God gives us the ability to produce it. However, we must avoid the deceitfulness of wealth. In a world that adores the rich and assumes the poor are cursed, we must be careful to reject the temptation to become arrogant and proud of our ability to acquire wealth. We should enjoy God's blessings when He delivers them and at the same time refuse to pat ourselves on the back and take up the value system of materialism. God's blessings are His gift to us that we must use as He intends. We must see ourselves or others, not more valuable because of wealth, but more responsible for God's possessions.

To do otherwise is to allow the deceit of wealth about which Jesus warned to choke out the Word of God (recall Matt. 13:22). This is the same as the temptation for Jesus to turn stones to bread—the temptation to chase after stuff instead of God's declaration. God's blessings are wonderful, and we must thank Him for them. But we must reject the materialism that tempts us to say, "This is what life is all about. I am the one who provides. See what I have done!"

Just like the prodigal son, we must come to our senses and embrace the generous grace of the Father. He is the one true provider. We are to enjoy the blessings but reject the temptation to position them as our highest value. Our highest value must be the Father's embrace. Everything else is a celebration of His provision.

When we can enjoy God's blessings without losing a proper value system and when we can enjoy our journey in the desert believing God trailblazes a safe path, we are learning to live on manna. We are choosing a Kingdom value system and seeking

God with our whole heart. We enjoy whatever material bless-ings He entrusts to us, but we value *Him*. Whether He leads us into times of scarcity or into times of plenty, we remain obedient because we value Him!

The Call to Transformation

As followers of Christ, we must confess where materialism is choking out the Word's ability to transform us. Our use of debt is killing our ability to help others, to tithe, and to maintain a balance between work and family. Materialism is infecting the church. Many churches evaluate success based on the budget rather than the number of people getting saved and experienc-ing transformation. We are raising a generation of people whose thirst for "stuff" is far more noticeable than their thirst for God. We must make a choice to return to the Father's house.

I would suggest this means we must embrace a few funda-mental commitments:

Commitment No. 1: We must take up our role as stew-ards rather than owners. We must make a fundamental de-cision about our relationship to God and material possessions. Psalm 24 lays a proper foundation for understanding this prin-ciple: "The earth is the LORD's, and everything in it, the world, and all who live in it" (v. 1).

There is absolutely nothing in our lives that we can claim as our own. We are only managers of God's resources. We are accountable to the owner for how we handle His "stuff." We cannot take any credit for what is in our possession. It is there by God's grace, and He can remove it without losing our trust and obedience.

Commitment No. 2: We must determine what we val-ue—God or money. As believers, it is vital that we reject the materialism of our day. Again, I want to be clear. I am not suggesting that having possessions is wrong. Materialism is the *worship* of "stuff." It is basing our life's direction, our value system, on the accumulation of things rather than on a proper relationship with God. We can have "stuff" and love God. But we cannot serve both (see Matt. 6:24). We are owned by one or the other. When our obedience is limited in any way by our commitment to accumulation, we are serving money. That arrogance chokes God's ability to lead us into the desert where we can be transformed by His discipline.

Commitment No. 3: We must determine when enough is enough. If God pours out so much blessing on us that we do not have room to contain it (Mal. 3), it makes sense that He has a purpose for the overflow. As followers of Christ, we must find out what God intends for us to do with the excess He entrusts to us.

A commitment to tithe the first 10 percent of whatever He trusts to our care is first. Tithing is not an option for a steward of God's possessions. It isn't a legalistic approach to money. It is a proper expression of trust in God's provision. This act of faith was practiced before the Law was ever given (Gen. 14:18-24), and it was promoted by Jesus as a part of our proper relationship to God (Matt. 23:23). It is neither legalism nor Old Testament Law. It is a universal act of worship and trust in God's provision.

However, our responsibility to be faithful stewards goes far beyond the issue of tithing. I would challenge you to determine what you need to meet the responsibilities in your life. You are accountable to care for the daily needs of your family (1 Tim. 5:8). That includes preparing for retirement. It also includes making decisions about how you will handle the educational needs of your children and maybe even your grandchildren. Yet there comes a point where enough is enough. Nobody can tell you where that point is. You must decide that with God before you reach it if you are to have any hope of resisting the temptation to hoard the blessing. God might be able to use you to do more than you ever thought possible if you just make the decision at the start.

Finally, we must determine what will become of any possessions we leave when we die. I would encourage you to consider tithing your estate to the Kingdom. That might include your local church, your denomination, a Christian foundation, a missionary effort, a Christian college, or any other number of Kingdom purposes. I believe we, not our heirs, are responsible for tithing the excess of our lives. I even believe that includes 10 percent of our life insurance. A brief meeting with an insurance agent and a signature is all that's needed to make sure your children follow your desire to honor God with this tithe of your last bit of income.

Commitment No. 4: We must follow God even when the journey requires more provision than we have received today. Many believers never experience the joy of living under the miraculous hand of God because they simply can't figure out how God is going to provide. They total the checkbook and know they don't have enough resources to do what God wants. They look at their stage of life and realize God's request just doesn't make sense at this time. They look at their calendar and can't figure out how to squeeze in God. So, like the rich young ruler, they go away sad.

We must choose a kind of faith that says, "I don't have to have the blessing in hand to know it is coming! God's blessings are endless, and He will provide all I need when I need it!" This isn't an excuse to avoid planning or to act in foolish disregard of good counsel. Jesus told us to count the cost (Luke 14:28-32).

His instruction wasn't intended as an evaluation of God's designs but as a call to evaluate our willingness to sacrifice. In the end, we must do what we know God is telling us to do, even when it costs us more than we think we can afford.

Commitment No. 5: We must model to our children "generosity" as opposed to "consumption." All of the events the children of Israel experienced when God delivered them from Egypt and led them to the Promised Land became opportunities to transfer their faith to the next generation. For instance, reenacting the Passover meal was one way to teach the children of future generations about what God had done (Exod. 12:26-27). It is our responsibility to raise our children to relate properly to God and His blessings. In a day when children crave the latest gadgets and television commercials tell us "we need more stuff," our responsibility to raise a generation that rejects materialism has never been more crucial. We must teach generosity rather than consumption. However, we must remember that these lessons are better caught than taught. Our children will become what we model.

Putting It All Together

We are tempted to believe the lie that the accumulation and consumption of stuff should be our highest value. The worship of abundance has even infiltrated the church. Instead of those who hold up provision and abundance as a means to bless God and others, we have modeled the materialism of our society. From churches that evaluate success on the basis of a balance sheet to believers who rob God of His tithe and ignore the needs of the hurting, we must repent of our materialism.

To embrace this call to live on manna means we must choose a completely different value system. As believers, we must rejoice for the material blessings God gives us and use those blessings to transform our world. We must always keep the commitment that "enough for today is enough for me." And we must be obedient and maintain a proper relationship to God and His blessings no matter what His provision is. We are safe whether He sends us a million dollars or a quarter, because we are in His house and all that is His is ours (even if we receive it in daily portions). We must not desire "stuff," but God. When He gives us "stuff," we rejoice, but we value Him.

5 THE QUESTION OF DESIRE

Do I Want Entertainment or Transformation?

Choose for yourselves this day whom you will serve, whether the gods your forefathers served beyond the River, or the gods of the Amorites, in whose land you are living. But as for me and my household, we will serve the LORD (Josh. 24:15).

The fourth question we have to answer, if we are to live on manna, is the question of desire. That is to say, if we are going to live under God's provision so that we enjoy His blessings but worship Him, we need to decide what we are really after. Do we want to be entertained by God's miracles or transformed by them? We can be entertained while watching from a safe distance, but we can only be transformed when we need God's intervention.

We have to choose whether we want to be spectators of God's miraculous work or participants in it. Many people only want to be entertained by God's miracles; they want to see God at work, but only if they can avoid any risk to themselves. However, if we want transformation, we must embrace a God who purifies us with fire. We must walk with Him through the valley of the shadow of death in order to really understand that there is no need to fear evil. We can watch others undertake that journey from afar, but we can only become more Christlike if we are willing to endure the trials that lead to transformation.

Do I Want to See Miracles or Experience Them?

The New Testament is filled with stories recounting the miracles Jesus performed. These stories telling of God's healing hand have helped hundreds of generations deepen their faith. We must not forget that many of the greatest faith stories are preceded by difficulty. The leper, the blind man, the lame beggar, the woman with the bleeding condition, the father whose child was dying, the little girl who was already dead, and even Lazarus all experienced the wonderful, miraculous provision of God. But their blessings sprang out of tragedy.

The leper had to endure not only the awful disease that wreaked havoc on his body but also the disdain and rejection of the society at large. The blind man had no way to take care of himself, nor did the lame man. The pain of a father losing a child, or a mother whose child is already dead, can barely be imagined.

The horrific reality is that God delivers His miracle as an answer to tragedy. That is where most of us cry, "Stop!" We want the miracle, but we don't want to experience the tragic circumstances that require the miracle. We want the manna, but we want it delivered to our dinner table while we enjoy the security of Egypt. We want transformation, but not the pain necessary to experience it. And so, we must make up our mind what we want more—entertainment or transformation. Most of the time we want the miracle, but we don't want to *need* the miracle. We must change our mind-sets. When we need the miracle, it isn't an evidence of being abandoned but a testimony that God is going to transform us.

Jim and Mary are wonderful believers who sacrifice a large part of their lives to service in the church. They love kids and are constantly involved in ministry to these dear ones. But their lives weren't always centered on Christ. The early years of a sinful life left Jim with an incurable form of hepatitis. His liver was so badly scarred that it was barely functional. Medications had no effect, and the doctors told Jim that his situation was so bad they wouldn't put him on a liver transplant list. Jim was as good as dead. The only question was how long he would have to endure the painful disintegration of his body.

Jim recognized the issues he was now facing stemmed back to poor choices and a life full of everything but God. But how could God allow him to go through this now—now that his life was centered and focused, now that he and Mary were living such good lives?

The physical issues were interfering with Jim's ability to work, and finances were slipping. The pressures grew along with the bills. Mary had faced some unexpected physical issues that caused her to lose work as well. The house they had built just a few years earlier was now a source of major stress because making each month's mortgage payment became harder and harder. They weren't sure if they were going to keep their truck either. "God, we could use a little help!" Their cries were getting louder and more desperate.

While our stories differ in detail from Jim and Mary's, we have all experienced those periods when nothing seems to be going right. We wonder how God could lead us through such dangerous territory. Doubts about God's faithfulness and our safety creep in and begin attacking the very foundations of our faith. During these times of desperation we have to decide what we really want out of life. Will we limit our obedience and faithfulness to only those times when life is enjoyable? Will we continue to follow God, even when we see no tangible evidence of His provision?

Jim and Mary's desperation grew so great that they asked the questions many of us have asked: "Is it really worth it? Does following God make any difference? If I am going to have to go through all of this, then shouldn't I just forget it and live for myself?" These are honest and brutal questions. Jim and Mary had to make up their minds whether they were going to follow God through the valley of the shadow of death.

Jim and Mary talked, prayed, and cried. And in the end, they committed themselves to following God no matter what. "We cannot turn back now. God is our only hope." Following God when you know you are going to win is easy. But Jim and Mary made the decision to follow God when all evidence said they were going to lose, and lose big. It is in this final surrender to live under God's provision, even when death is certain, that we find God's ability to transform our hearts.

Mary said, "I finally came to the point where I looked at the truck and said, 'I don't need that truck.' I even realized if God wanted to take our house away, that was OK by me." The days weren't easy. Jim's body would just shut down on a moment's notice. His joints would ache so much that he could barely get out of bed. But they had made their decision. They would walk with God through this valley. They would not run for cover. God was with them and His provision would be enough.

The church gathered around Jim and Mary in prayer. They were anointed for healing as they prepared themselves for the difficult days ahead. Regardless of how God chose to heal Jim, through a miracle or death, they were God's and they refused to deny Him.

As if all of these problems weren't enough, Jim fell and cracked a rib while working. He and Mary went to the emergency room, and the doctor took X rays. As the doctor went over the film with Jim, something unexpected happened. Jim mentioned his damaged liver in the middle of the conversation. "There is nothing wrong with this liver," the doctor replied. Jim corrected him. "My liver is full of cirrhosis. It has been that way for years. I barely have any function left." The doctor replied, "I'm looking at this picture of your liver, and I don't see any abnormalities at all."

When Jim met with his family physician a few days later, the doctor was adamant: "Something isn't right here. Your liver is damaged. I've seen your previous pictures. There is no way your liver is perfect. That would have to be a miracle. I've only seen that two times. There is no way your liver is OK." So they set up an appointment for an ultrasound to get an accurate picture of what was going on.

The ultrasound confirmed the miracle. Jim's liver was perfect. Jim and Mary had experienced the miraculous hand of

God. God had reached into Jim's sick body and had restored health where no doctor could. The miracle was just in time, and just enough. It didn't fix the financial problems. Mary's physical issues continued. However, God's provision was complete.

Jim's liver was not the only thing changed. Mary and Jim had come face-to-face with a fundamental question of the soul: "Will I serve God even if He slays me?" (see Job 13:15). When they answered yes, they found a transformation of the heart that was no longer panicked at the prospect of having nothing. The source of their peace had shifted from their possessions to their God who provides. Jim understood the psalmist's words, "Even though I walk through the valley of the shadow of death, I will fear no evil" (Ps. 23:4). Jim had come to realize that peace doesn't come from the miracle. It comes before the miracle. Peace comes because of God's presence. The miracle is icing on the cake. Jim's peace came when he thought he only had a few months to live.

That is wonderful news for those who experience God's provision without healing. Another dear lady who attends church with Jim also struggles with a failing liver. She has lived on heavy doses of medication for over ten years. Her testimony is also one of faith. She says, "I don't know why God doesn't just heal my liver too. But He did provide for me. My liver works enough to keep me going. I'm not dying. I take an awful lot of medicine every day. But I have to thank God for how He has taken care of me."

Each of these people understood that living on God's provision is the source of peace. Whether or not that provision takes the form of complete healing, God's ability to provide and protect through the valley of the shadow of death is sure. And so we find the faith to endure the trial and to grow closer to God through it.

Transformation Comes Through Hardship

When we decide that our primary desire is to be like Christ, we must accept the reality that transformation usually comes through hardship. The writer of Hebrews encourages us to welcome these times as God's way of bringing our character in line with His—it produces holiness and peace. The secret is to set the focus of our eyes (what we desire) firmly on Christ. I can endure the hardship because my desire is to be more like Him. I choose to see whatever difficult day God leads me through as an opportunity for transformation.

Therefore, since we are surrounded by such a great cloud of witnesses, let us throw off everything that hinders and the sin that so easily entangles, and let us run with perseverance the race marked out for us. Let us fix our eyes on Jesus, the author and perfecter of our faith, who for the joy set before him endured the cross, scorning its shame, and sat down at the right hand of the throne of God. Consider him who endured such opposition from sinful men, so that you will not grow weary and lose heart.

In your struggle against sin, you have not yet resisted to the point of shedding your blood. And you have forgotten that word of encouragement that addresses you as sons:

"My son, do not make light of the Lord's discipline,

and do not lose heart when he rebukes you,

because the Lord disciplines those he loves,

and he punishes everyone he accepts as a son."

Endure hardship as discipline; God is treating you as sons. . . . Our fathers disciplined us for a little while as they thought best; but *God disciplines us for our good, that we may share in his holiness. No discipline seems pleasant at the time, but painful. Later on, however, it produces a harvest of righteousness and peace for those who have been trained by it.* (Heb. 12:1-7, 10-11, emphasis added)

What's Our Focus?

If we are to endure hardship, we must embrace the idea that God's discipline is a good thing. That is not natural. All of us have resisted the discipline of our own parents and authority figures. At our core, we want entertainment, not transformation. That has to change.

Our desire to reflect Christ's character must become the very focus of our heart. We need to set our eyes on the "author and perfecter of [our] faith." We can be like the Pharisees, who stood on the sideline watching the activity, or we can jump into the baptismal waters and declare once and for all, "I'm all in!"

Setting our focus on Christ means seeing ourselves as the object of His transformational work: "He is the author and perfecter, and I am the one He is working on." So we need to let Him take us on difficult journeys where His discipline leads to a heart of holiness. If we want to be like Christ, we have to allow Him to lead us into dangerous territory.

The Gift of Trials

When the attention of our hearts shifts to a desire for Christlikeness and we accept that transformation comes through hardship, we will see difficulties as a gift from God. There is no need to accuse God of abandonment. He hasn't forgotten us. He cares enough to walk with us, to lead us, to transform us through our trials.

I love and hate this all at the same time. I love that God is going to transform me but hate that it is going to hurt. The writer of Hebrews honestly admits this (12:11). However, I embrace the process because of the harvest of righteousness and peace it produces. I have learned to pray something like this: "God, teach me whatever You need to teach me. And teach me quickly. I don't want to stay here any longer than I need to. So, if You are going to take me through this painful period, I welcome it. But help me learn fast." This attitude is what the writer of Hebrews is referring to when he says, "It produces a harvest of righteousness and peace *for those who have been trained by it*" (v. 11, emphasis added).

Trials become periods of transformation, not just because they are difficult, but because we expect God to use them as opportunities to produce righteousness and peace. There are many people who enter times of difficulty and aren't transformed. Their attention strays from Christ, and they begin accusing God of abandonment. But that is not how we have been instructed to deal with times of difficulty.

We are to keep our desires aimed at becoming more like Christ. So our difficulties are filtered through this expectation of transformation. It might take some time to get over the shock of being blindsided by life. But in the end, we must come back to our senses and ask God to use our trials as discipline. Peace comes because we have fully incorporated the truth that God hasn't abandoned us just because the pathway has become treacherous. God is going to teach us something, and we need to stay close to Him to learn it. We can't learn it from afar as a spectator. We have to learn it on the journey, following the Shepherd's voice.

Will I Follow Him into Dangerous Territory?

So the question becomes, "Will I follow the Shepherd into dangerous territory? Am I willing to let Him lead me through the valley of the shadow of death?" The imagery of Ps. 23 is that of a shepherd watching over the daily care of his flock. It is a picture of our relationship with God when life gets dangerous. We are safe because of God's daily provision:

The LORD is my shepherd, I shall not be in want.

He makes me lie down in green pastures,

he leads me beside quiet waters,

he restores my soul.

He guides me in paths of righteousness

for his name's sake.

Even though I walk

through the valley of the shadow of death,

I will fear no evil,

for you are with me;

your rod and your staff,

they comfort me.

You prepare a table before me

in the presence of my enemies.

You anoint my head with oil;

my cup overflows.

Surely goodness and love will follow me

all the days of my life,

and I will dwell in the house of the LORD forever.

Ray Vander Laan shares a fascinating look at Ps. 23 in his book *Echoes of His Presence*. His insights help us understand how God's provision and protection work. The "green pastures" of Ps. 23 were nothing more than patches of grass that grew up in rocky places. They were sparse, and if a shepherd allowed a flock to stay in one place, the resources would quickly be used up and the sheep would starve. So the shepherd would lead his flock through a treacherous journey from grassy spot to grassy spot. If the sheep would wander off to find their own food, they would likely starve. They couldn't see far enough ahead to know where the next spot of provision would be. Moreover, they didn't know where their journey should lead. If left to their own understanding, they were as good as dead.

The mountain pathways were treacherous. Steep cliffs on one side and thorny thickets on the other meant the shepherd had to stay in front of the sheep, walking on the path he wanted them to follow. If the sheep left the pathway laid out by the shepherd, they could easily become trapped in the thickets and be easy prey for predators. Their sight was so bad they could easily get too close to the edge of a cliff and simply fall to their death. The shepherd's guidance and leadership, his rod and staff, was critical.

When the evening came, the shadow of the mountains made walking these pathways that much more dangerous. These walks through the "valley of the shadow of death" required the sheep and the shepherd to pay special attention. So the shepherd would move close to the sheep so that they could hear his voice and see where to follow. If they didn't listen and watch, they could easily plummet to their death. (Laan, 1996, pp. 27-29)

There are some important realities to keep in mind as we choose to let God lead us into dangerous territory. First, God isn't leading us into danger to harm us. The grassy spots we need can only be found as we travel the path through dangerous territory. He is taking us into days of trial on purpose. We can't see far enough ahead to know why we are going this way. But we must trust His love for us enough to believe He is taking us there for our good. If we panic and abandon His leadership, we are dead. We can't see as well as He sees. We don't know where the danger lies. When we're setting our own direction, we might feel that we have more control. However, our self-direction has placed us in perilous danger. It is imperative that we turn around and follow the shepherd.

Second, even though the provision looks spotty, God knows how to make sure we don't run out. We can complain and scream at God, "I can't believe You would ask me to live on this little bit of grass! Look at it. It can barely make it up through the rocks. Don't You care enough to give me more than this?" Or we can enjoy today's provision and continue to follow God as He leads us to the next spot of grass. We choose to trust that He knows what we need and that if we continue to follow, we will always have enough.

Finally, when life gets really rough—when the darkness of our circumstances starts casting shadows so thick we can't even see the edge of the path—that is when we must draw close to Christ and not abandon His leadership. These most difficult hours are when we learn we are safe because of His close leadership, not because we can instruct Him how to lead us.

I have faced this temptation to instruct Him more than I care to admit. When life gets tough, really tough, I panic: "God, I'm not telling You what to do here, but here's what You need to do. And You need to do it quickly!" I am like the sheep that is confident the Shepherd was supposed to take a hard left at the last bush. I bawl and bawl. "Not this way! Not this way!"

We have to decide whether we will turn around and show Him the pathway He was supposed to take or whether we will resist the urge to take over. Who is in charge? If we assume the role of leader, we will surely die. But when we maintain the role of follower, we learn He can lead us through the valley of the shadow of death. There is no need to fear evil because the shepherd is guiding us. His rod and staff (His pushing and pulling) keep us from walking off the cliff. He knows the way. Our job is to stay close and listen.

The journey can be very stressful as we learn to trust God

through the shadows. My wife and I have often laughed through the pain: "I know the Bible says God will never let us be tempted beyond that which we can bear. But I wish God didn't trust us so much!" Even in the last few years as God has been teaching us that He can be trusted to provide, the learning has been painful. This book is the result of learning to trust God through days of scarcity. As I was forming these ideas and sharing them with my wife, she expressed her reluctance for this kind of learning, saying, "I wish God would teach us how to stay faithful to Him on a million dollars! I would enjoy a book about that." We laughed because we knew it was true. It would be wonderful if God could transform us through bounty. But it just doesn't seem to work that way.

When we make up our minds that we would rather look like Jesus than be comfortable, we are ready to participate in the transformational miracles of God. We will then allow Him to take us into dangerous territory because we trust that He is taking us there for our own good. He will train us and transform us. The more He transforms us, the more He can use us. Righteousness and peace are going to be the bounty He produces in us because we are willing to walk with Him through the valley. When we look at our difficulties and see them as opportunities for this kind of transformation, we are ready to listen to God's voice as He provides the answer to our need. This is when provision (manna) becomes sweet.

6 GOD'S ANSWER
The Sweetness of Provision

The people of Israel called the bread manna. It was white like coriander seed and tasted like wafers made with honey (Exod. 16:31).

Daily Provision Is Bittersweet

Is it really possible that the terrifying journey of living on daily provision could become "sweet to taste"? When resources are always "just in time" and only "just enough," when relationships require more effort than we feel we can give, when our energy levels could not possibly be drained any further, and when one of a thousand other variables in life leave us absolutely dependent on God for survival, maintaining an attitude that accepts trials as good is more than difficult. It almost sounds ridiculous to believe that this can in any way leave a pleasant taste in our spiritual mouths.

Yet I would suggest that as we embrace God's design, we will learn that daily dependence opens us up to the Holy Spirit's power to transform our lives. In this transformation, though the discipline and trial we endure are bitter, daily provision becomes bittersweet. It is bitter because we are required to let go of the pretense of self-protection and self-preservation. But it is sweet, because giving up our dependency on anything but God's daily provision teaches us that living on manna is a powerful force of transformation in our lives.

So when difficult circumstances blindside us, we are no longer trapped in the belief that we are powerless victims. Because we are living on manna, God's ability to provide assures us of victory. It is in the powerful act of hope-filled faith that we can enjoy the sweet transformation of the Holy Spirit.

A Powerful Tool for God

From trial to trial, the power of the Holy Spirit is unleashed in our surrender to His provision. And so, with each morning's discovery of manna on the lawn, our joy deepens. We are being transformed into vessels He can use—even under extreme pressure. We are becoming powerful tools in the kingdom of God.

We don't have to have the blessing in hand to follow God on the journey. We don't have to know where the end of the journey is to believe God has a set direction. We don't have to know what tomorrow holds to maintain our peace, and we don't have to know where the resources are coming from before we sacrifice them. We live on manna! God is our provider and protector. Today's need for provision is another opportunity for God to empower us for ministry. And so the provision becomes honey on our tongue.

Choosing to See Provision as Pleasant

There are many ways we experience the sweetness of provision. I want to focus on four: (1) the sweetness of God's ability, (2) the sweetness of peace, (3) the sweetness of God's protection, and (4) the sweetness of transferred faith. As we look at these areas, keep in mind that we make a choice to interpret God's provision as something to be enjoyed or something to be rejected. When we cling to provision's power to transform us, we enjoy it. When we resist provision as risky, we reject it.

We see this in the attitudes of the children of Israel. They had lived under the daily provision of God and were now being asked to take one last step of faith into dangerous territory. It was time to take the Promised Land, to step into the blessing of God. While the land was flowing with milk and honey and produced a bountiful harvest, it was also occupied by giants.

Moses had sent scouts into the land for an honest assessment of the situation, and they returned with their report. The scouts agreed on what they had seen but disagreed on the Israelites' capacity to possess God's promise. The first group believed God would deliver the land into the Israelites' hands. They believed in God's provision. They had been trained by living on manna. The other group believed the people dwelling in the Promised

Land had the upper hand. Even though this group had enjoyed the manna, they had refused to be transformed by the experience. Their lack of faith would shatter their hope of provision.

They gave Moses this account: "We went into the land to which you sent us, and it does flow with milk and honey! Here is its fruit. But the people who live there are powerful, and the cities are fortified and very large. . . .

Then Caleb silenced the people before Moses and said, "We should go up and take possession of the land, for we can certainly do it."

But the men who had gone up with him said, "We can't attack those people; they are stronger than we are." . . .

Then Moses and Aaron fell facedown in front of the whole Israelite assembly gathered there. Joshua son of Nun and Caleb son of Jephunneh, who were among those who had explored the land, tore their clothes and said to the entire Israelite assembly, "The land we passed through and explored is exceedingly good. If the LORD is pleased with us, he will lead us into that land, a land flowing with milk and honey, and will give it to us. Only do not rebel against the LORD. And do not be afraid of the people of the land, because we will swallow them up. Their protection is gone, but the LORD is with us. Do not be afraid of them." (Num. 13:27-31; 14:5-9)

The Sweetness of God's Ability

Manna isn't sweet because there are no trials. There were giants in the land. They weren't going to just lay down their weapons and walk away. To posses the land God had promised meant the children of Israel were going to have to overcome some pretty serious obstacles and face many dangerous situations.

Both groups who spied out the Promised Land understood this. The difference wasn't that one group recognized the challenges and one group didn't. However, the group who understood the sweetness of manna knew that their hope was in God's ability to provide, not in their ability to defeat an enemy.

When we choose to see our victory as dependent upon our ability, we run the other way. But when we have been trained to trust God's daily provision, God's ability to overcome any difficulty is part of what makes manna sweet to the taste. We have confidence in God's ability to provide. So the dangerous territory we now face is nothing less than another opportunity for God to provide. We are confident in His provision.

The Sweetness of Peace

Joshua and Caleb called on the children of Israel to fix their eyes on God's ability and not on the problems along the journey. They were honest about what happens to our hearts in decisions like this. When we choose to give our attention to the problems, we rebel against God and live in fear. However, when we choose to believe our success rests in God's ability, we can lose the fear and experience peace.

That is not to say we enjoy the battles we must fight. It doesn't mean our knees quit shaking. There will be days along the journey when we will want to crawl in a hole and hide. There will be periods when our faith will face massive testing. There will be days when we will turn to God seeking assurance that He has not abandoned us.

Peace that comes from confidence in God's ability brings our troubled hearts back into a state of hope: "Yes, I'm afraid of giants. But God is bigger. Yes, this is going to be tough and it is going to hurt. But God is able. Yes, I'm in over my head. But God isn't. I'm OK."

The Sweetness of Protection

I love Joshua's confidence: "We will swallow them up. Their protection is gone" (v. 9). We look at the details of our circumstances and honestly admit, "I don't know how God is going to do it, but I know He is going to do it. He didn't call us here to abandon us. If He told us to take the land, then the land is already ours for the taking!" It doesn't matter what God has called you to, there will always be giants in that land. There will always be obstacles bigger than you. However, they are not bigger than God. We are confident in our victory because God has already given us the land. His provision is sweet. We are protected, even in battle.

The Sweetness of Transferred Faith

The generation who refused to see God's ability to overcome obstacles would never enter the Promised Land. It would take a generation who knew nothing of Egypt to finally trust God's provision enough to take the Promised Land. But let's not forget their faith was developed watching their parents struggle to trust God's provision.

God was getting ready to lead Joshua and the next generation across the Jordan to take the Promised Land. God had promised to provide a land flowing with milk and honey, but the parents couldn't get past their lack of faith. The Scriptures say, "So [God] raised up their sons in their place" (Josh. 5:7).

We must understand the wonderful truth that our children learn to trust God as they walk with us through the desert times. Their faith is being formed just as much as ours. When we remember that they are watching us and learning whether or not God can be trusted, our faith for the trial is emboldened. We are reminded that we are to pass along this faith in God. The generations to come will need to know they can trust God to provide all they need for whatever He calls them to accomplish. Like the Passover feast or the stones removed from the Jordan's riverbed, our faith stories become hallmark moments that teach the generations to come that God can be trusted to provide.

Early Lessons Pay Great Dividends

When we choose to follow God through days of daily dependence, living on manna, we and our children learn to embrace God's ability, His peace, His protection, and the faith that is being transferred from one generation to the next. The blessings we receive will be for both us and our heirs.

In chapter 2 I wrote of my parents' early days of faith development and the excitement they expressed as God revealed His ability to provide. They had learned that difficulty was the avenue through which miracles come. It had become an exciting journey of absolute dependence. God would use those early faith lessons to provide the strength they would need to serve God.

Dad accepted a call to preach and took his first church in Rockton, Illinois. The church was small, but it didn't matter. The God who had provided in the past was the same God who would provide for their needs now. They had gained a confidence in God's ability to provide. And so they embarked on the journey with every expectation that God would meet their needs.

It didn't take long before my parents realized just how much they were going to need God. Dad made sixty dollars a week. He worked side jobs to put food on the table. He loved the Lord and was sacrificing to advance the Kingdom.

However, finances were getting worse, and Christmas was coming. Mom and Dad prayed together for God's intervention. They knew peace comes because of God's presence. Rather than run from the trial, they drew close to the Shepherd.

We were getting ready to go to school when Mom and Dad called us into the kitchen. They explained that we needed to pray. The cupboards were bare. The only thing in the house was a can of green beans. My parents knew that during the dark shadows the most important thing we could do was to carefully follow the Shepherd's leading. So we gathered around the table, joined hands, and prayed.

"God, we don't have anything to eat. We need Your help. We know that You are able to provide for our needs, and we know that You know what is going on. But, God, we need to come to You today as a family. We need You to know we are counting on You. We know somehow, someway You will protect us." After this, my brothers and I headed to school.

Don and Elaine Turner pastored a sister church just a few miles away. Later that morning they paid an unexpected visit to Mom and Dad. Dad and Don sat at the kitchen table while Mom and Elaine sat in the living room. Mom and Dad were so grateful for the fellowship. There is something about conversation with friends that makes difficult days more palatable.

Don asked Dad to help carry in something from the car. Mom heard the commotion from the other room but didn't pay much attention. After several rounds of the front door opening and shutting, Mom's curiosity peaked, and she asked, "What are they doing?" Elaine said, "Well, let's go and see." As they went into the kitchen Mom's jaw dropped. The table we had prayed around was now filled with bag after bag of groceries.

"Our church adopted you for the holidays," Don explained. "As we were gathering funds for missionaries, we were also gathering these groceries for you!" It was manna! God had been providing the resources before my family ever knew we would need it. Rev. Turner continued, "Now Christmas is coming and some folks from the church will be dropping off some gifts for you and the boys."

Mom and Dad knew the faith lesson four little boys needed to learn. This was also part of the sweetness of manna. And so the groceries stayed right there where God had provided them—on the kitchen table where we had gathered for prayer just hours earlier.

We learned something about the "sweetness of manna" that day. After school, the closer my brothers and I got to home, the heavier the memories of our early prayer meeting weighed on our minds. As we walked in the front door, we came face-to-face with God's capacity to bless those who remain faithful. We were astounded as we saw the smiles on our parents' faces. Joy and peace filled that little parsonage as Mom and Dad told us how God had provided.

We couldn't fit all the groceries in the cupboards. Groceries were literally stacked up on the counters. "I will . . . pour out so much blessing that you will not have room enough for it" (Mal. 3:10). We hadn't memorized the scripture, but God wrote it on our hearts that afternoon. We knew we could trust God, even when we couldn't see how He was going to provide. Lessons like that can't be learned in the safety of a Sunday School class. They are learned as we hold God's hand and walk into the unknown territory of unrestricted obedience.

It is all about who He is. He delights in providing manna when we call to Him. It is in these kinds of moments, when we approach a difficulty as an opportunity for a miracle, that the manna becomes pleasantly sweet.

More than You Could Ever Ask or Imagine

Christmas was coming and Mom and Dad knew this dear congregation would be bringing presents. There was a knock at the door, and there they stood, presents in hand. Mom and Dad graciously invited them in. These dear folks were as excited as we were, but they were confused by our lack of surprise. "Aren't you surprised that we are here?" they exclaimed. "Well, your pastor told us you were coming," replied my dad. The group was quite disappointed. "He wasn't supposed to give away the surprise," they said. Then they laughed and enjoyed our celebration of the sweetness of God's provision.

In the middle of his conversation with them Dad mentioned the groceries. "What groceries?" they said. Dad responded, "The groceries your church gathered for us. Your pastor dropped them off. That's when he told us you were coming." "Our church didn't gather any groceries," they replied. "Which church do you attend?" Dad asked. They weren't from Don's church at all. And then, everyone realized just how much God had provided. God had also laid our family on the heart of another church! God knows our need and cares more about our hearts' desires than we could ever believe. He is providing for us in ways and through people we can't begin to presume.

It would have been justifiable before my parents received all this provision for them to accuse God: "God, we are serving You with all we have. How is it that You could abandon us like this? We're down to a can of beans here! Christmas is coming, Lord. What are we going to say to these children?" But they didn't. They had learned so many years before that these times of scarcity are God's opportunity to bring about His miracles. He provides manna when we need it. This was a time to call out to God, not accuse Him. Our family had learned that manna is sweet because God can be trusted to provide.

Passing Along a Heritage of Manna

Because my parents handled their adversity with that kind of faith, my brothers and I learned something valuable about the trustworthiness of the Blessing Giver. We learned to call out to God in our scarcity. We learned that a lack of resources doesn't mean resources aren't at our disposal. We learned to anticipate the hand of God rather than question His faithfulness.

This is part of the sweetness of manna. Where difficulties could become the source of a spiritual meltdown, they become a source of spiritual expectation. God uses these challenging times to build into us a character of hope that looks to heaven with expectation rather than accusation.

These early memories of the sweetness of manna gave me the courage to follow God into dangerous territory years later. That's the way it is. When we accept the training manna provides, it becomes a powerful tool of transformation. Like David in front of Goliath, we face our giants by recounting the many ways in which God's provision has proven sufficient (1 Sam. 17:34-37).

Learning these kinds of lessons is brutal. My brothers and I couldn't have learned them without the pain and anxiety of having nothing. I am often tempted to beg God to protect my own children from such scarcity. But then I must admit that they will not learn the lessons about God's ability to provide until they are forced to call out to God in the midst of need. I know I could not handle life's problems if I had not learned God is able to move beyond my circumstances. As much as my knees still shake when adversity hits, I am learning to enjoy the sweetness of the peace and courage being formed in my children.

As I began my ministry at Segue Foundation, I was finishing up some pro bono work I had done for a church. Income was sparse, but we were confident we were following God's call. On one particular Sunday, I sat with my family in church and began writing our tithe check. My children were watching. They knew how tight finances were. My youngest leaned over and whispered in my ear, "I thought we didn't have any money." I replied, "This isn't my money. It's God's." My answer made sense, and he dropped the issue.

I leaned over to my wife and whispered, "You see that check? That's all the money in our checking account. God's going to have to provide." She looked at me with that "this is scary, but I trust God" kind of honesty. She gripped my hand, nodded in agreement, and then we worshipped.

At lunch that day, we called out to God for protection. Diana looked at the boys and explained it was going to be a tight week. "You know the tithe check Dad wrote this morning?" They nodded. "We gave God what was His. That is what we should do. We don't rob God. We trust Him to provide. But there isn't any money left after our tithe. So we are going to trust God and not whine. There isn't going to be any eating out or anything extra for a while. But God is going to protect us." Our prayer for dinner was fervent as God was preparing my boys' hearts to learn something about living on manna.

Two days later, I had a planning meeting with the church I had been helping. We were getting ready to kick off their Enduring Gifts Ministry. Twelve months of work were coming to fruition. It was so exciting to see God working in this church. As I walked out of the meeting and headed to my car, I thanked God for letting me be a part of what He was doing. I was reaching to open my car door when I heard a voice calling from the church. I looked up to see one of the members standing in the doorway.

"Kevin, can you come back in for a minute." I walked with this gentleman down the hallway where the pastor and one other member were standing. "We wanted to tell you how much we appreciate all you've done to help us." They handed me an envelope. "It's not much, but we wanted to say thank you."

I thanked them and headed to my car. When I opened the envelope, the amount of the check was within a few cents of the tithe check I had placed in the offering on Sunday.

I was so excited. But the excitement had little to do with the balance in my checkbook. I had two boys at home who were going to see the hand of God at work. I knew this was one of those sweet manna moments where their faith in God was going to grow.

I rushed in the door and yelled, "Boys! Come here! I want to show you what God did today!" They came in wide-eyed. "What happened?" they said. "Do you remember when we prayed at Sunday lunch and asked God to take care of us?" I replied. "Yes," they said, sensing something was coming.

I pulled out the check, laid it on the table, and told them what had just happened. Their jaws literally hung open. This is when the transformational power of living on manna turns to honey on the tongue! It was time to pass on the faith. "I want you boys to remember this day. I want you to know you can trust God to provide, even when you don't know how!" They picked up the check, patted me on the back, and said, "God sure came through, didn't He, Dad?"

Choosing Sweet Manna

In that moment, I realized why my parents chose to endure such days of trials while trying to raise four little boys. Walking through the valley of the shadow of death can be sweet. It is the only place we learn there is no need to fear evil. Again, that is why I do not beg God to keep my children from having to endure the same kind of scarcity I had experienced. I came to realize the sweetness of needing God's miracles. Faith grows deep under that kind of absolute dependence.

I think this is what James is getting at when he instructs us in chapter 1 of his Epistle: "Consider it pure joy, my brothers, whenever you face trials of many kinds, because you know that the testing of your faith develops perseverance. Perseverance must finish its work so that you may be mature and complete, not lacking anything" (vv. 2-4).

Trials are times of sweet provision when we interpret them as pathways to maturity. They are times when our faith and the faith of our children grow in ways that wouldn't be possible if everything were easy.

The cost of an easy life is far too great. If we never need God to perform the miracle, we never experience the miracle. There is so much to be gained when I am willing to walk with God on treacherous paths. I embrace the journey of manna because God walks with me, and I am confident He is using this time to build me into a usable vessel.

Once we have fully bought into the idea that God really is there, that He really does care about us and cares about our needs, something happens to us. What once terrified us becomes sweet to the taste. What once caused us to question whether or not God had turned His back on us, now becomes the powerful period of transformation into His likeness.

Shaking Knees, Steady Hearts

It is not that our knees quit shaking when we face days of difficulty but that we no longer look to heaven wondering if we are alone. We have moved from the terror of self-dependency to the power of God's provision. We are steadied by the anticipation of God's miraculous hand and the resulting peace that comes from absolute confidence in His ability to provide. We begin to understand what Paul meant when he said he had learned to be content in all circumstances—in want and in need. Like the children of Israel, we are able to wake up in a desert, with no way to provide for ourselves, and yet still experience every morning the delicious feast of honey-tasting manna.

It is in moments like this that we must also resist the temptation to accept every option in front of us as God's provision. Not everything that looks like manna is manna. In Josh. 7, the children of Israel are depicted overthrowing kingdoms in the Promised Land. They were instructed not to take any silver or gold for themselves, but some were tempted to use this as an opportunity to provide for themselves a source of provision outside of God's plan. In the end they paid with their lives.

Our temptation is similar. We are tempted to use sources of safety outside of God's plan. We even can go so far as to blame it on God: "God gave me the credit card, so I used it." "Surely God doesn't want me to be unhappy. He knows I need this." It is so easy in the middle of a trial to accept any option as God's provision.

When our knees are shaking, we must search the Scriptures, turn to prayer, seek wise counsel, and be very careful about the choices we make. A steady heart comes from both the Holy Spirit, as well as the spiritual support we find in Christian brothers and sisters.

God's Provision Brings Hope

Steve and Lori Fehlinger are good Christian people who love the Lord. However, their story is one of tragedy and faith. God's daily provision led them through the pain and grief of losing two children. It also led them into the blessing of their daughter Hope and son Shane.

Lori was pregnant with their first child. Their church family celebrated with them as they looked forward to God's little blessing. However, their journey would soon take them into the valley of the shadow of death.

Both this pregnancy and the one that followed failed. Steve and Lori endured the pain of losing two children. Both children were born whole and complete, but they had passed on to heaven's gate before they could draw their first breath.

There are no words that can soothe the heart of a mother who has lost two children. However, her church family became the daily manna God would provide. They prayed, sent cards, and gave hugs. They came to the hospital and walked with Lori during the hours and days to come. "Who would do that?" Lori asked with a kind of thankfulness I did not expect from someone who had experienced such tragedy. "My church family would!"

Most of us in this kind of situation would be more than tempted to reject the idea that God cared at all. But Steve and Lori turned to God's provision of manna. Lori explained how she made it through those dark days: "My church family members were the first people I thought of and the first place I ran."

Her testimony is astonishing to any who have struggled to understand God's benevolence in such loss. "I grew closer to God during those days," declared Lori. Lori's choice to open herself to God's provision had given her the peace and confidence to continue walking with God through the valley. God would be faithful.

Steve and Lori decided to adopt. Once again their church family gathered around them in times of prayer and encouragement. It was Easter. Steve was playing the trumpet, and Lori gave a testimony of God's love. After the 8:30 service their phone rang. It was the hospital. The birth mother was in labor.

Steve and Lori enjoyed the miracle of watching their daughter, Hope, come into the world. Lori shares the amazing awe of those moments: "It was one of the most amazing days of our life. To be with God on Easter Sunday with our church, who had been through everything with us, and then to experience the birth of a live child. . . . the crying was the most beautiful music to our ears!"* They named her Hope. God had provided and they brought Hope home.

Many people would never choose to see their trial the way Steve and Lori did. They would have shaken their fist to heaven and accused God of not being faithful. But Steve and Lori had chosen to joyfully receive the provision of manna God supplied through their church family. They chose a heart of thanksgiving and adoration. And in the end, God provided in an unforeseen way the answer to their hearts' cry.

The Miracle Goes On

Wouldn't you know it! A short time later, Steve and Lori got the unexpected news. She was pregnant again. What should have been an absolutely joyful realization was filled with anxiety. Would it happen again? It was true that God was their protector and provider. He would give them whatever they needed to make it through the journey. But would He allow them to come home with their son?

As hard as she tried, Lori suffered under the awful potential of another failed pregnancy. She trusted God. That wasn't in question. But she faced these days with shaking knees and a burdened heart.

One Sunday as Lori headed into the sanctuary to prepare for worship, her small-group leader stopped her. "Lori," he said, "God told me on Saturday that I was to tell you not to worry. He just told me to tell you not to worry." He hugged Lori, and she and Steve headed into the sanctuary.

---

*Steve and Lori Fehlinger, interview by author, video recording, September 2007.

Even now Lori still isn't sure why Steve didn't take them to their regular seat in the sanctuary. But for some reason, they sat on the other side of the church. Lori was getting ready for worship when she noticed a piece of paper sticking up out of a Bible in the pew. Lori decided she would take a look after the pastor finished his sermon.

The pastor finished preaching and Lori took the pew Bible and opened it to the slip of paper. It was at Matt. 6:25. The first words Lori read were a gift of manna: "Do not worry." Lori testifies to God's provision, "I knew at that time God was telling us our son was going to come home. And he did. Shane came home and joined our family!"

God of the Details

It never ceases to amaze me that the God who holds the entire universe in His care is capable of orchestrating even these tiny details. He cares enough to have some unknown person place a slip of paper in a pew Bible so that He can reassure us that everything is OK. He keeps the galaxies in place but cares enough about our needs to handle details such as these.

We must choose the kind of faith that believes in the loving hand of God and His ability to care for our needs, however large or small they might be. This kind of faith makes daily provision sweet. Yes, living on manna is frightening at times. No, we never get so used to it that our knees quit shaking along the narrow paths of the journey. But our hearts find peace in the middle of the shadows because He is with us and we choose to trust His voice. "I am here. I will not abandon you. Do not worry."

It's Your Choice

When Jesus taught us to pray for daily bread, He was instructing us to choose an attitude of daily dependence on God.

That call will either become a frightening source of uncertainty and instability, or it will become a powerful tool of transformation. As you choose to see God's daily provision as a bit of honey-tasting manna, the Holy Spirit will empower you with the kind of faith that steps into the river and expects it to divide.

7 SPIRITUAL TRANSFORMATION
Ready to Take the Land

Be strong and courageous, because you will lead these people to inherit the land I swore to their forefathers to give them (Josh. 1:6).

Transformed Through the Journey

Why is it that some people seem to be able to come through adversity with a great faith while others are spiritually destroyed? Those with great faith look to heaven and ask for God's help. Those who are spiritually destroyed look to heaven and accuse God of being untrustworthy.

God is able to use those who choose great faith to conquer battles that would destroy others. When we have answered the questions of living on manna and have chosen to trust God's daily provision, we are choosing great faith. God is now able to use us to transform our world. We are able to enter dangerous territory where we would die without God's intervention. We do so with peace. Miracles are on their way, so we can expect to be victorious.

This was the defining difference between the adults who left Egypt and never entered the Promised Land and their children who did. While adversity destroyed their parents, the children chose great faith. The children lived their entire lives in absolute dependence on the provision of God, and it transformed their character. They watched their parents struggle. They saw God provide for the faithful and strike down the disobedient. Provision was a daily reality, and they had no picture of life without God's miraculous intervention.

While the journey could have left them cynical, their decision to be obedient to God's plan was an indication that living on manna had built their faith. This is the generation who would transform their world. They would walk into dangerous territory with an absolute trust in God's ability to bring miraculous victory.

Forty years earlier their parents decided God could not overcome the people occupying the Promised Land. Even though they had experienced God's ability to overcome Pharaoh's army, had seen God part the Red Sea, and had been living on manna, they were still unsure God could be absolutely trusted. But now the children stood on the shores of the Jordan and with great faith answered God's call to move into the land of milk and honey. They had been transformed by living on manna, and they were ready to take the land.

As we look into our own hearts and try to find the strength to follow God through our own days of adversity, we will find it helpful to take a look at the spiritual transformation evidenced in the generation who possessed the Promised Land. By looking at the changes in their hearts, we find a beginning place to seek God's transformation of our own hearts.

Their story is recorded in the Book of Joshua. While there is not time to complete a full study of this amazing story, a quick survey of some of their major spiritual transformations will help us set the stage for our own search for victory. There are several key transformations I would suggest are critical for us to develop the kind of faith that can follow God into the dangerous territory of victory.

An Obedient Spirit

First, they had an obedient spirit. Joshua is ready to lead the children of Israel across the Jordan. God has called them to go. But this generation will have to decide whether they are going to follow God's leading. Their response indicates the kind of obedience to God's call they had chosen: "Then they answered Joshua, 'Whatever you have commanded us we will do, and wherever you send us we will go'" (Josh. 1:16). They had learned the crucial lesson that they were safest when they were following God's commands.

As we ask God to transform our faith, we must choose the level of our obedience *before* we enter dangerous territory. We cannot face days of extreme trial, where resources are only enough to make it through the day, if we have not fully devoted ourselves to God. However, when our obedience has been settled, God can trust us to face giants and not run away.

Not Distracted by Abundance

The second generation had experienced another transformation. God could trust them with abundance. They would not shift their worship from the Creator to His creation. They were able to receive the abundance of Canaan's harvest without abandoning their absolute dependence on God. In Josh. 5, when this generation ate of Canaan's produce, the manna stopped. God trusted them with the abundance of Canaan. God could do this because their hearts were committed to worshipping Him as their only provision (Josh. 24:16).

We must be able to enjoy the blessings of God, even in abundance, without losing the attitude of daily dependence. We must resist the temptation to tightly hold on to our material blessings as our source of safety. When we choose to completely surrender ourselves to God's provision, we can enjoy the abundance and use it for God's purposes without becoming disobedient to His design.

Only Worship God

The children of Israel had to give up their dependency on the god of materialism. Where the first generation turned to a golden calf in the middle of their panic, the second generation had resolved to worship God alone:

Joshua said to the people, "You are not able to serve the Lord. He is a holy God; he is a jealous God. He will not forgive your rebellion and your sins. If you forsake the Lord and serve foreign gods, he will turn and bring disaster on you and make an end of you, after he has been good to you."

> But the people said to Joshua, "No! We will serve the LORD."
>
> Then Joshua said, "You are witnesses against yourselves that you have chosen to serve the LORD."
>
> "Yes, we are witnesses," they replied.
>
> "Now then," said Joshua, "throw away the foreign gods that are among you and yield your hearts to the LORD, the God of Israel."
>
> And the people said to Joshua, "We will serve the LORD our God and obey him." (Josh. 24:19-24)

This transformation is one of our most difficult spiritual victories. God needs to be able to trust us to keep our worship focused on Him alone. In a culture that values the accumulation of stuff over all else, we must decide what we will worship—God or His creation. When we have abandoned this culture's value system of materialism, God is able to trust us in times of plenty and want. When our obedience isn't dependent on whether we have more than we need, or not enough for most people to survive a day, we stay faithful to the call of God to walk forward in His plan. Where others would abandon the journey for an easier path, we continue to follow the Shepherd's voice.

Deal with Sin Quickly

The third transformation the children of Israel experienced had to do with their intolerance of sin. They took their sin seriously and confronted it quickly. In Josh. 7, as mentioned earlier, Joshua and the children of Israel confronted a family who had disobeyed God's command. One family had kept part of the spoils of a battle, something God had strictly prohibited. Joshua's army lost the next battle. When God revealed that the loss was due to disobedience, Joshua's actions were swift and severe. The offending family was stoned and burned.

While I am not suggesting that we stone anyone who sins, we should note how committed to absolute obedience the entire assembly of Israel had become. All of Israel but one family had followed God's command faithfully, and they dealt with that family swiftly.

The call to transformation is clear. If God is going to use us to transform our world, we can no longer tolerate partial obedience in our own lives. We must take our disobedience seriously. We understand that God is the One who gives us victory, and we cannot afford to choose up sides with His enemy. We must allow God to search our hearts and confront us with those areas where we have chosen anything less than complete obedience.

No Plan Bs

There is another area of spiritual transformation that can be seen as Joshua divides the Promised Land among the people. Much of the land had not been fully conquered. But as an act of faith, Joshua assigned different territories to different families.

There were some who had not fully possessed the land God had given them. Rather than admit that their fear of those who occupied the land was keeping them from obeying God's call to take the land, they asked Joshua for another option. Once again they were trying to create a "plan B" to replace God's perfect will:

The people of Joseph said to Joshua, "Why have you given us only one allotment and one portion for an inheritance? We are a numerous people and the LORD has blessed us abundantly."

"If you are so numerous," Joshua answered, "and if the hill country of Ephraim is too small for you, go up into the forest and clear land for yourselves there in the land of the Perizzites and Rephaites."

The people of Joseph replied, "The hill country is not enough for us, and all the Canaanites who live in the plain have iron chariots, both those in Beth Shan and its settlements and those in the Valley of Jezreel." (Josh. 17:14-16)

God had called the people to possess the land and yet some were battling the same temptation their parents had battled years earlier. They wanted to observe God's miracle without enduring the pain that comes when we go on the journey. This attitude was no longer tolerable for this people of faith. Joshua confronts them straight on. "But Joshua said to the house of Joseph—to Ephraim and Manasseh—'You are numerous and very powerful. You will have not only one allotment but the forested hill country as well. Clear it, and its farthest limits will be yours; though the Canaanites have iron chariots and though they are strong, you can drive them out'" (vv. 17-18).

We must take to heart the lesson they had learned. Even when we have received the abundance of the Promised Land, we cannot fall prey to the temptation to choose the easy road. Many times God's will leads us through difficulty. We are tempted to find an easier path. However, we will have to realize that we may very well have to drive out our "Canaanites" before we can fully possess all God has for us.

When God lays out His will for our lives, we must follow His plan. Yes there will be obstacles to overcome. However, we cannot let the difficulties we will face keep us from moving forward. If God called us, He will provide the resources we need to fulfill His call. When our hearts have fully bought into this reality, we are ready to take the land.

Ready to Take the Land

It took a generation who only knew absolute dependence on God's provision to finally take the Promised Land. This generation knew their safety was to be found in God's ability to win the victory. They had to fight battle after battle to take the land. The journey didn't get easier but more difficult. And yet, they heard God's call to move forward and they obeyed. Straight into danger, they obeyed.

When we make up our minds to follow God, regardless of the dangers involved, life doesn't get easier. It can get very difficult. Forces aimed at our spiritual destruction don't just give up and walk away. Gaining spiritual victory is going to require a fight. There are going to be some strongholds that seem larger than we can handle. We will face our own giants, our own walls of Jericho, our own battles to the death.

However, when we have placed our absolute trust in God's ability to provide, refused to worship other sources of safety, quit demanding that God provide more than today's resources, and embraced the painful reality that transformation comes through the trial, God is able to start breaking down strongholds in our lives.

Commitments of a Transformed Heart

We are now ready to take the land and that is going to mean facing some pretty serious battles. There are some very important commitments we must hold if we expect to stay faithful to God when He leads us into dangerous territory.

Commitment No. 1: We must be willing to start the journey without knowing where God is taking us. God calls us to follow Him, and we no longer have to know the itinerary in order to obey. Like Abraham, sometimes God calls us to follow Him into uncharted territories. When we can follow Him there, He can use us to break down strongholds.

Commitment No. 2: We must be willing to attempt the impossible. Many times God calls us to do things we know are beyond our ability. However, we know all things are possible with God, so we move forward anyway. We must be confident that God is able and that we are not. And in that sober judgment, we gain confidence that God will accomplish the impossible through us.

Commitment No. 3: We must be willing to obey even when it doesn't make sense. Many times, God calls us to deal with issues that are beyond our understanding. Sometimes God's directions don't make sense. "Why should I walk around Jericho every day for a week? Why should I shout after a long day of walking? I don't know, but God told me to walk and shout and that's what I'm going to do." That kind of obedience experiences the joy of watching impenetrable walls crumble under God's provision.

Commitment No. 4: We must be willing to run into danger where others would run away. God's call can be frightening. When we understand that He leads us into dangerous territory to transform us, we must be willing to move with Him into days that would cause others to run. Yes, we should count the cost. However, counting the cost is the process of letting go of anything that would hinder our obedience. If we are to take the land, no cost can be too high. Like the man who sold all he had to buy the field with a hidden treasure (Matt. 13:44), we count the cost and decide the journey is worth all we have.

Commitment No. 5: We must be willing to attack obstacles when others would give up. Where others would look at those opposing them and cry out, "I can't defeat these giants," we look and believe that God has already taken away their strength. The size of the opposition has no relationship to God's ability to bring victory. If God said, "Go take the land," we know in our hearts there are no giants large enough to stop us.

Commitment No. 6: We must be willing to sacrifice when others would hoard resources. Like the children of Israel who gave up the spoils of the battle, we must resist the temptation to believe life is only about accumulation. We will enter into days that require sacrifice because we are committed to God, not materialism. We exude a life of generosity, hinged on the commitment to tithe and supported by a heart willing to help those in need.

Commitment No. 7: We must be willing to stay on the journey. We must not allow ourselves to get lost in the desert. We hear God's call to take the Promised Land, and we are no longer willing to have anything less than His complete will. We choose obedience rather than excuses and stand firm in the battles that obedience brings. We have lived on manna and have been transformed by it. God is our provider, and we intend to do His will, no matter what.

I watched my father keep these commitments while going through some difficult days of the journey. I was a sophomore at Olivet Nazarene University, and my parents pastored a small church in Illinois. The church had a history of running off pastors, but my parents had enjoyed wonderful relationships and their ministry was strong. For a while, it looked as if they had been able to take the church into new territory. They would soon find out there were still some battles to fight before the Promised Land was truly won.

When the old sin showed its head, things got ugly. A few members joined together in an all-out attempt to destroy my father's ministry. On a weekend visit home, I witnessed the extent of the battle firsthand. A man I had respected for many years was now standing in the foyer of the church screaming at the top of his lungs. He was hurling accusation after accusation while my father stood and took it with a level of grace I had never before witnessed. I was amazed and stunned. I was amazed at the level of control my father was showing, and I was stunned at how vicious the battles we fight can become.

Later that afternoon I asked my father an honest question. "Why do you stay here and put up with that? You are a wonderful pastor and could get a church anywhere in the country. You don't have to do this!" He was obviously far deeper into the journey of daily dependence than I could comprehend at that point in my life. He said, "Everything in me wants to run away. I didn't create these problems. They were here before I got here. But God has asked me to stay. If I leave, how will this church ever find their way past this pattern of sin?"

It was a commitment level that made no sense to me but would become a stronghold of my faith later on. Dad stayed through the dangerous and difficult days of the journey. His courage allowed his church board to finally call an end to the sinful behavior. Because of a pastor who wouldn't run away and a board that was willing to stand up for what was right, the church found transformation. Years later those who had behaved so poorly came back to my father and asked for forgiveness. The church had finally taken the Promised Land, not because the journey was easy, but because spiritual leaders trusted God to stand with them in the battle. The costs were counted, the sacrifices deemed worthy, and God provided the victory.

Ten years later I sat in my office in the middle of my own battle for the transformation of a very young and vulnerable congregation. I had stood up for what was right, and I was facing attacks as a result.

I was deep in prayer begging God to get me out of that situation when the Holy Spirit intervened: "Kevin, remember the faith of your father." It was a simple statement that brought a flood of pictures through my mind. I saw my father standing in the fire during his days of battle. I remembered the healing and the sense of joyful fellowship that had overtaken that congregation as they overcame their problems. I sensed the Holy Spirit telling me, "If I helped your father through days like that, I can help you with these battles as well." The Holy Spirit was calling me to cross my own Jordan. The Promised Land would be taken. The battles would be real, but victory was certain.

I was learning that stepping into God's victory isn't for the lighthearted or those who are easily shaken. Victory in dangerous territory takes faith that has been transformed by daily provision. Victory requires commitments few others are willing to make. However, if we are willing to traverse the dangerous territory of God's provision, victory is certain.

Circumcision of the Heart

The commitments required for victory are not easy. They will require more spiritual strength than we can deliver on our own. It is going to take the power of the Holy Spirit to deliver these spiritual transformations to our hearts and these commitments to our minds. He is going to have to circumcise our hearts.

While the adults Moses circumcised had not required this obedience of their own children, Joshua demanded it before they went into battle (Josh. 5). The second generation allowed themselves to be circumcised. This was more about a commitment to absolute obedience than a mark on the body. They were solidifying their commitment to be God's children.

Paul teaches us that circumcision is representative of what must happen in our hearts if we are to obey God: "A man is not a Jew if he is only one outwardly, nor is circumcision merely outward and physical. No, a man is a Jew if he is one inwardly;

and circumcision is circumcision of the heart, by the Spirit, not by the written code" (Rom. 2:28-29).

The Holy Spirit needs to cut away anything in our lives that is not surrendered to God's leadership. When this happens, God can trust us to fight for victory and not abandon Him. We will stay faithful to God during times of plenty and times of want because we have chosen to worship the Creator over His creation. He is what we want. Our hearts are His alone.

This can be seen in the hearts of this second generation, the generation of great faith. Listen as the children of Israel respond to Joshua's call to serve only God in the Promised Land:

> Then the people answered, "Far be it from us to forsake the LORD to serve other gods! It was the LORD our God himself who brought us and our fathers up out of Egypt, from that land of slavery, and performed those great signs before our eyes. He protected us on our entire journey and among all the nations through which we traveled. And the LORD drove out before us all the nations, including the Amorites, who lived in the land. We too will serve the LORD, because he is our God." (Josh. 24:16-18)

As followers of Christ, we understand this declaration of faithfulness can only be kept through the power of the Holy Spirit. I need the Holy Spirit to give me an undivided love for God if I am going to be able to stay faithful to Him when life gets tough. The Holy Spirit needs to transform my heart so that Christ's character is reflected in me. I cannot overcome the forces that battle my faith without such a circumcision of my heart.

Transformation Means Looking like Jesus

Paul teaches us what it means to live with a transformed heart in the middle of a culture whose value system is not holy. In Eph. 4 and 5 Paul spends considerable time calling us to become imitators of Christ in a world corrupted by "deceitful desires." An untransformed heart is marked by a continual lust for more and more of the things that are opposed to God, and this greediness Paul calls idolatry in 5:5. Listen as Paul begins his call to transformation:

> So I tell you this, and insist on it in the Lord, that you must no longer live as the Gentiles do, in the futility of their thinking. They are darkened in their understanding and separated from the life of God because of the ignorance that is in them due to the hardening of their hearts. Having lost all sensitivity, they have given themselves over to sensuality so as to indulge in every kind of impurity, with a continual lust for more. You, however, did not come to know Christ that way. (Eph. 4:17-20)

If God is going to be able to change our hearts so that we reflect Christ, He is going to have to change the way we think. Paul lays out a picture of the way we think before our hearts have been transformed by the Holy Spirit. We are separated from God and have a lust for more and more of the things that He opposes. Our hearts are hardened and our thinking is futile. We have so bought into the idea that life is about consumption, getting more and more of the many things we lust after, that we cannot accept a God who calls us to sacrifice. To the world, life isn't about giving away all we are but is about getting all we can.

While Paul's teaching deals with far more than money and wealth, his warning is firm. Do not buy into a value system that preaches life is about getting all you can. That "continual lust for more" (v. 19) is not a reflection of the God who gave His life so that we could live. If we are to grow under the leadership of the Holy Spirit, our hearts must be circumcised of such a value system.

We were taught a gospel that calls us to a different mind-set: "You were taught, with regard to your former way of life, to put off your old self, which is being corrupted by its deceitful desires; to be made new in the attitude of your minds; and to put on the new self, created to be like God in true righteousness and holiness" (4:22-24).

We have already seen that the deceit of wealth, the mind-set that says accumulation is what life is all about, is a part of the deceitful desires to which Paul is referring. This idolatry of greed has nothing to do with a heart of true righteousness and holiness. The heart of righteousness and holiness says, "I want my character to reflect the sacrificial love of Christ." Or in the words of Paul, "Be imitators of God, therefore, as dearly loved children and live a life of love, just as Christ loved us and gave himself up for us as a fragrant offering and sacrifice to God" (5:1-2).

A Model of Sacrifice

What has the journey of living on manna taught us? The journey is about transformation. That transformation isn't aimless. We are called to reflect God's holiness in our character. Paul defines that as living a life of love after the sacrificial model of Christ. In the same way Christ gave himself up for us, our lives are to be about giving, not taking. We are to live a life of love, not a life of greed. We are to give ourselves up as a fragrant offering to God. That means if He calls us to live in abundance, we will not fall prey to the idolatry of greed. It means that if He calls us to live in want, we will not fall to the temptation of accusing God of withholding His blessing. We have been circumcised in the journey of living on manna. Our hearts are focused on loving God and God alone.

To love is to sacrifice. Jesus said it: "Greater love has no one than this, that he lay down his life for his friends" (John 15:13). This is the life of sacrifice Paul calls us to in Ephesians. Again, it is the life of giving, not taking. The transformation of our hearts from greedy to generous is critical. And when we let go of the old way of thinking, our hearts are being prepared to walk into days of victory as God delivers the Promised Land into our hands. He is able to use us to confront a world of darkness. We can handle the fight because our hearts have been transformed. We don't live our lives as an act of accumulation but as a sacrifice to God.

If this is the case, we must heed Paul's warnings: "But among you there must not be even a hint of sexual immorality, or of any kind of impurity, or of greed, because these are improper for God's holy people. . . . For of this you can be sure: No immoral, impure or greedy person—such a man is an idolater—has any inheritance in the kingdom of Christ and of God" (Eph. 5:3, 5).

We must reject the idolatry of greed. Life cannot be about how much we get but about following God's will regardless of the cost. Anything less is tarnished by a value system in which we love stuff more than God. God wants to use us to transform our world. He cannot do so until we have been transformed in our thinking and have rejected the idolatry of greed.

Wise Living in an Evil World

If we are going to be able to live this life of love, then we must be constantly aware of how this world's value system is try-ing to penetrate our thinking and behavior. Paul counsels, "Be very careful, then, how you live—not as unwise but as wise, making the most of every opportunity, because the days are evil. Therefore do not be foolish, but understand what the Lord's will is" (vv. 15-17).

It is possible to begin our victorious march into God's plan for our lives and then fall prey to the foolish and evil patterns of the world around us. We must be careful. The days we live in are evil. This world does not accept daily provision as blessing and is constantly challenging our understanding of abundance and safety.

We are constantly bombarded with the call to worship stuff. One credit card company's commercial lays out this culture's call to abandon living on manna. It says, "I want it all! I want it all! And I want it *now!*" Embracing an attitude of daily provision will require that we live carefully and recognize that while we are journeying in the Promised Land of God, there are still battles to fight and enemies of our soul to defeat. The victory is ours if we are willing to make the commitment of a transformed heart.

Daily Provision, Continual Filling

However, Paul is clear about the role of the Holy Spirit in keeping our hearts in a right relationship to God: "Be filled with the Spirit" (v. 18). Paul is not simply talking about a one-time filling but a continual filling. We are to be continually filled with the Spirit. We are able to live a life of love, where generosity rather than greed marks the way we handle abundance, because we are constantly being filled with God's Holy Spirit.

Again, being ready to take the land, to walk into days of spiritual victory, does not mean there are no more battles to fight. On the contrary, we have been transformed by daily dependence so that we can fight the battles that victory requires. Jesus called us to pray for the attitude of living on manna because it is the only way our hearts can be prepared for victory. When we can experience the abundant blessings of God without being tempted to worship the creation over the Creator, when we can experience the desert journey where enough for today is enough for us without accusing God of abandonment, and when our worship and surrender to the Holy Spirit is experienced as a daily continual filling, God can use us to overcome obstacles, defeat enemies, and participate in His miraculous provision of victory.

Manna in Everyday Life

As we finish this look into Jesus' call to live on manna, it is important to recognize that it is difficult. Do not be surprised if the very realization that God wants us absolutely dependent on Him creates more questions than answers. I want to conclude this study by addressing some questions people just like you and I have asked as they have grappled with the prayer for daily bread.

Manna and Relationships

Many people have asked questions about how living on manna relates to our obligation to take care of our families. Scripture teaches us clearly that we are to take care of their needs (see 1 Tim. 5:8). However, there are a couple dangers we must avoid as we follow these instructions.

First, we must refuse to place our safety in the hands of anyone but God. We are often tempted to look at our family and believe they have a responsibility to keep us safe. They need to make enough money, have the right attitude, do the right thing, and so on. When they don't, we believe we are in danger.

If we are to keep God as our only source of safety, we must resist the temptation to believe that anyone but He keeps us safe. We need to talk with each other about our concerns. We are to work together to lay solid plans as we have prayed for guidance. However, when we believe that our spouse, our children, our boss, or anyone else keeps us safe, we have made "gods" out of them.

Second, we must refuse to see ourselves as their "messiah." As we fulfill our call to take care of our family's needs, it is easy to forget that God is the One who provides the resources we will need to complete the task. As much as we must do all that is within our strength to care for their needs, we are not God.

Many times the best thing we can do for our loved ones is to go with them to the foot of the Cross and ask for God's help.

Manna and Generosity

If we are going to follow Jesus' call to living on manna, we must take on a life of biblical stewardship. I dealt with the issue of tithing at many points throughout this book. However, it is important enough to restate the issue here as we deal with the practical, day-to-day issues of living on manna.

We will never understand the joy and freedom of dependence on God until we have abandoned our worship of money. We must practice tithing the first 10 percent of our income to God as the first step to walking away from materialism. It is not legalism, or Old Testament law. Jesus taught tithing with a heart of mercy. In a generation where the effectiveness of the church to reach our world is being hindered by the financial disobedience of the community of faith, we must repent of our materialism, quit robbing God, and worship God through our generosity.

Manna and Sabbath

I was in the middle of one of those prolonged times of testing when living on manna is more than a figure of speech. The difficult days had lasted well over a year, and I was honestly exhausted. I was getting ready to make dinner for my family, and everything in me just wanted to crawl in bed and hide from the world.

I uttered an honest cry to God: "God, I am so tired of living on manna. I need a break. I need some time to just enjoy life and not deal with all of these issues." God's response was quick and quiet: "You need Sabbath." And then it struck me. It is no wonder God demanded the children of Israel to observe a day of rest. They had been working seven days a week for years. They didn't know how to stop. But when we are living the exhausting journey of absolute dependence, it is imperative that we stop and rejuvenate our souls.

It is tempting to get so wrapped up in life that we fail to take time to refill our spiritual tanks. Many people even go to church and never have Sabbath. Sabbath is a time for us to stop the train and get off. We are so good at filling our schedules beyond the breaking point. But when life is tough and the trials are hard, we cannot afford to continue pouring out our hearts without replenishing the soul. We must remember that even Jesus took time to get alone with God. If Jesus needed this time with God, it is pretty safe to assume we do to.

Does God Want Me in Poverty?

Although God does not pour out the same level of financial abundance on everyone, God does not intend for everyone to live in poverty. God even warned the children of Israel to not forget Him when He blessed them with houses and land. He told them that He was the One who gave them the ability to acquire wealth. As mentioned previously, the call is to avoid the deceitfulness of wealth that tries to convince us that our safety is to be found in the blessing rather than in the Blessing Giver.

Manna and Financial Planning

Earlier I referred to 1 Tim. 5:8 in which Paul instructs us to take care of our family's needs. Some might begin to think that embracing Jesus' call to live on manna means we should not plan for such things as retirement or our children's education. I would suggest to you that taking care of our family's needs also means planning for future needs.

There is nothing spiritually wrong with getting prepared to meet your family's needs during retirement. There is nothing wrong with planning for the expenses of college. Leaning on God's ability to provide also means using resources He has made available for us to plan ahead. That is not unspiritual. It is smart.

The question we each have to ask is, "How much is enough?" God blesses us so that we can meet the needs of our family. However, He may also bless us beyond their needs. It is our responsibility to prayerfully determine how He would have us use the overflow to impact the world around us.

There is another issue that we must address as it relates to living on manna and financial planning. Living in absolute dependence on God's provision doesn't give us permission to make foolish financial choices. I am still required to be a faithful manager of God's resources. Do not forget that the manager who was unfaithful with the blessing entrusted to him was stripped of his possessions (Matt. 25:14-29). While I am convinced God is faithful to help us clean up the messes we create, that doesn't mean we should recklessly abandon common sense. Those who are faithful with little will be trusted with much.

Do I Ever Get Used to Living on Manna?

I am frustrated by my own tendency to still panic when life gets tough. I think most believers would admit the same. It might be that there are a few giants of the faith who never freak out at life's trials, but the majority of believers would have to honestly admit living on manna is always tough. About the time we think we've got the battle of our emotions won and we will never doubt God again, life blindsides us. We look around and begin wondering if we are going to survive. We look to heaven and once again scream, "God, You've got a problem."

Embracing the pattern of daily bread does make a difference though. We have a core belief that steadies our hearts. In the middle of our panic the Holy Spirit whispers in our ear and reminds us there is no need to fear. It might take some time, but this value system that accepts God as our only trusted resource brings our panic under control. We regain the assuredness of our faith, and we continue following Christ through the trial.

I wish Jesus had instructed us to pray, "Let us live in the Promised Land." Wouldn't that be great? There would be no more need for daily provision. Why couldn't it be that a day would come where we would no longer be required to desperately need God for survival?

However, Jesus instructed us to continually include in our prayers the request for daily bread. As much as I wish the journey of absolute dependence would end, it does not. We will not come to a place where we are strong enough to make it without God. We will never enjoy the day when we possess everything we need for tomorrow's challenges. We will always need more from God than we have right now.

However, as we are transformed in the journey of living on manna, we learn to enjoy being participants in God's miracles. We learn that spiritual transformation only happens as we walk closely with the Shepherd. It is during the dark days of walking through the valley of the shadow of death that we learn to listen for the Shepherd's voice. We also learn that no matter how dark the shadows of despair might appear, we are safe under His leadership.

Like the children of Israel, we will be tempted to turn to other sources of safety for our provision. We will be tempted to shift our worship from the Creator to His creation. We will be tempted to trust our own ability to provide over God's. We may even be tempted to believe God has left us as the journey gets difficult.

However, we have chosen to have great faith. It is a faith that chooses to look for transformation in the trial; that chooses obedience, even when it is difficult; and that refuses to value the blessing over the Blessing Giver. It is a faith that only worships God and recklessly overcommits to God's "plan A." As we incorporate great faith into our response to God's call, God will use us to transform our world. Whether in plenty or want, we are choosing to live on manna.

CONCLUSION

We have heard Jesus' call to pray, "Give us today our daily bread." As much as we wish this call was a call to an easy life, we understand it is a call to an attitude of absolute dependence on God's provision. The journey can be very frightening as we struggle to answer the core questions of manna: "Do I really believe God is there and cares about me? Do I trust Him as my only source of safety? Is enough for today enough for me? Do I want to be entertained by the miracles or transformed by them?" We are willing to engage these issues because we are tired of simply being entertained by God's miracles. We want to participate. We want to be transformed!

When we come out on the other side and have abandoned the value system of materialism, we understand that dependence on God is sweet because it leads us to the powerful transformation of the Holy Spirit, where spiritual victory becomes possible. Peace, even in the midst of trials, is found in His presence, not the abundance of material possessions. Our obedience can be fully expressed in both times of plenty and times of want. Neither abundance nor scarcity distract our obedient worship of the Creator. He is our manna, our provision, and we will only worship Him!

And so, we come before the Holy Spirit and ask Him to circumcise our hearts. We relinquish our disobedience, our need for accumulation, our plan Bs, and our sinful worship of the creation over the Creator. We fully commit ourselves to becoming more and more like Christ and welcome our need for the daily provision of God's Holy Spirit. We live out the life of love modeled by Christ in which generosity is expressed through sacrifice, and we reject the continual lust for more that has entrapped our world in the idolatry of greed.

It isn't an easy journey. There are many dangers and many battles. But none of that is foreign to us. We know what it is to exhaust our resources at the end of the day only to wake up to the miraculous provision of manna. Our inability won't stop us. Our lack of resources won't defeat us. God is our manna and He has transformed our faith. Our victory is certain. We are a people transformed by *living on manna.*

BIBLIOGRAPHY

Butler, Trent C. 1998. Word Biblical Commentary [computer file]: *Joshua*. Ed. David A. Hubbard, Glenn W. Baker, John D. Watts, and Ralph P. Martin. Electronic ed. Dallas: Word. 304 pp. (Logos Library System).

Christensen, Duane L. 1998. Word Biblical Commentary [computer file]: *Deuteronomy 1—11*. Ed. David A. Hubbard, Glenn W. Baker, John D. Watts, and Ralph P. Martin. Electronic ed. Dallas: Word. 223 pp. (Logos Library System).

Dictionary of Biblical Imagery [computer file]. Gen. ed. Leland Ryken, James C. Wilhoit, Tremper Longman III; consulting ed. Colin Duriez, Douglas Penney, Daniel G. Reid. Electronic ed. Downers Grove, Ill.: InterVarsity Press, 2000, ©1998. xxi, 1,058 pp.: ill.; 26 cm. (Logos Library System).

Dictionary of Jesus and the Gospels [computer file]. Ed. Joel B. Green and Scot McKnight; consulting ed. I. Howard Marshall. Electronic ed. Downers Grove, Ill.: InterVarsity Press, 1997, ©1992. 993 pp. (Logos Library System).

Dictionary of New Testament Background [computer file]: *A Compendium of Contemporary Biblical Scholarship*. Ed. Craig A. Evans and Stanley E. Porter. Electronic ed. Downers Grove, Ill.: InterVarsity Press, 2000 (Logos Library System).

Durham, John I. 1998. Word Biblical Commentary [computer file]: *Exodus*. Ed. David A. Hubbard, Glenn W. Baker, John D. Watts, and Ralph P. Martin. Electronic ed. Dallas: Word. 515 pp. (Logos Library System).

A Greek-English Lexicon of the New Testament and Other Early Christian Literature [computer file]: *A Translation and Adaption of the Fourth Revised and Augmented Edition of Walter Bauer's Griechisch-deutsches Worterbuch zu den Schrift en des Neuen Testaments und der ubrigen urchristlichen Literatur* by William F. Arndt and F. Wilbur Gingrich. Electronic ed. of the 2nd ed., rev. and augmented. Chicago: University of Chicago Press, 1979. Published in electronic form by Logos Research Systems, 1996 (Logos Library System).

The Greek New Testament [computer file]. Ed. Kurt Aland, et al. Electronic ed. of the 3rd ed. (Corrected). Federal Republic of Germany: United Bible Societies, 1997, ©1982. 926 pp. (Logos Library System).

Hagner, Donald A. 1998. Word Biblical Commentary [computer file]: *Matthew 1—13*. Ed. David A. Hubbard, Glenn W. Baker, John D. Watts, and Ralph P. Martin. Electronic ed. Dallas: Word. 407 pp. (Logos Library System).

The IVP Bible Background Commentary [computer file]: *Old Testament.* John H. Walton, Victor H. Matthews, and Mark W. Chavalas. Electronic ed. Downers Grove, Ill.: InterVarsity Press, 2000 (Logos Library System).

Laan, R. V. 1996. *Echoes of His Presence.* Colorado Springs, Colo.: Focus on the Family Publishing.

Lincoln, Andrew T. 1998. Word Biblical Commentary [computer file]: *Ephesians.* Ed. David A. Hubbard, Glenn W. Baker, John D. Watts, and Ralph P. Martin. Electronic ed. Dallas: Word. 494 pp. (Logos Library System).

New Dictionary of Biblical Theology [computer file]. Gen. ed. T. Desmond Alexander and Brian S. Rosner. Electronic ed. Downers Grove, Ill.: InterVarsity Press, 2001 (Logos Library System).

Smith, Ralph L. 1998. Word Biblical Commentary [computer file]: *Micah-Malachi.* Ed. David A. Hubbard, Glenn W. Baker, John D. Watts, and Ralph P. Martin. Electronic ed. Dallas: Word. 358 pp. (Logos Library System).

Strong, James. 1995. *The Exhaustive Concordance of the Bible: Showing Every Word of the Text of the Common English Version of the Canonical Books, and Every Occurrence of Each Word in Regular Order* [computer file]. Ontario: Woodside Bible Fellowship. 1340, 262, 127, 79 (Logos Library System).

Theological Dictionary of the New Testament [computer file]. 1985. Ed. Gerhard Kittel and Gerhard Friedrich. Trans. Geoffrey W. Bromiley; abridged in one volume by Geoffrey W. Bromiley. Electronic ed. Grand Rapids: William B. Eerdmans. Published in electronic form by Logos Research Systems, 1996. 1,356 pp. (Logos Library System).

Throckmorton, Burton H. 1921. *Gospel Parallels-NRSV* [computer file]: *A Comparison of the Synoptic Gospels.* Ed. Burton H. Throckmorton Jr. Electronic ed. of the 5th ed. Nashville: Thomas Nelson, 1997, ©1992. 212 pp. (Logos Library System).

STUDY GUIDE

Following Christ into days of adversity or scarcity can be frightening. Learning to trust God's ability to take care of you during days like that isn't easy and takes time. There are many lessons to learn and many questions you will need to answer before daily dependence becomes the normal response of your heart. However, you are beginning that journey and God will be faithful.

The following questions are intended to help you reflect on the issues raised in each chapter of this book. As you read the chapters and answer these questions, ask God to begin transforming your faith. As you pray the Lord's Prayer, asking for daily bread, allow your heart to embrace the call to live under the miraculous hand of God. Such a position is frightening and exhilarating all at the same time. As God teaches you the safety of absolute dependence, He will deliver a peace that can only be learned while living on manna.

Chapter 1 Questions

1. Have you ever experienced a time when the resources you needed were suddenly gone? What was your first reaction? What kinds of things did you say to God?

2. One a scale of 1 to 10 with 1 being "not at all" and 10 being "I will die without Him," how much do you need God to make it through today? What challenges does that create for you to trust God with the resources you need?

3. Have you ever had a time when you failed miserably? How did you turn to God during that time? How were you tempted to run from God during that time? What lessons did this time teach you?

4. The author says, "We enjoy provision. But we detest *daily* provision." Can you remember a time when God provided "just enough, just in time"? What was most difficult about that experience? In what ways was obedience to God difficult or easy?

5. The author says the most difficult emotional decision is answering the following question: "Just because God provided for us today, can we trust Him to come through again in the morning?" Why do you think this is so difficult for so many people? What parts of this are most difficult for you? What advice would you give to someone wrestling with this issue?

6. When are you most tempted to trust the blessing over the Blessing Giver? Why? What parts of the blessing are most tempting for you to trust over God?

7. What are some of the plans you put in place just in case God fails to come through? What do you think God would say about having a "plan B"?

8. Does dependence on God tend to invigorate or terrify you? Why?

9. Do you tend to wonder "if" God is going to come through or "how" God is going to come through? In what ways is God stretching you to trust Him more?

10. The author says, "We must refuse to allow our trust in God to be determined by the abundance of the provision." In what ways is your trust in God determined by how much He has already provided for you? How difficult is it for you to trust God for those things He hasn't yet given you?

11. The author says there are four questions that have to be asked and answered (p. 21). Which of the four seem most difficult for you? Why? Which seems easiest? Why?

Finish the prayer below:

Lord, as I am learning of Your call to live on manna, help me to
. . .

Chapter 2 Questions

1. When is it most difficult for you to really believe God is carefully paying attention to your needs? How do you deal with those times?

2. If you really believed God is your one provider, how would you change your spending habits? In what ways would this affect your tendency to worry? Would this impact the level of your generosity? Why? Why not?

3. The author says, "When we run after the blessings instead of the Blessing Giver, we never gain peace." Do you agree with this statement? Why? Why not?

4. Can you think of a time when you honestly called out to God with a "desperate persistence"? In what ways were you tempted to accuse God of abandoning you? In what ways were you able to maintain a sense of trust in God?

5. The author says that God's "attention isn't diverted by the complexity of our circumstances. He isn't panicked by the severity of our need. His resources aren't stretched by our apparent poverty." Is it easy or difficult for you to believe this when life is difficult? Why? What do you think God would say to you about how you handle days of adversity or scarcity?

6. When has God's presence given you hope when others would have given up? What lessons did you learn from those times? What advice would you give to someone who is feeling hopeless?

Finish the prayer below:

Lord, I am learning to trust Your care for me, even when life is difficult. I know You see my need and never quit watching over me. This week please help me with . . .

Chapter 3 Questions

1. What are the top three sources of safety you turn to when life gets tough? Why do you think these are the things you tend to trust for safety?

2. In what ways has God challenged you to place your sense of safety in Him? What changes will need to happen in order for that to take place?

3. Have you ever experienced a time that challenged your willingness to trust God no matter what? What lessons did that time teach you?

4. In what ways has God provided for you in uninvited and even unwanted ways? How difficult was it to accept God's design for your safety?

5. In what ways was God providing in unseen ways? How long did it take you to realize God has provided an answer? In what ways did this change your understanding of God's provision?

6. Deuteronomy 32:10 reminds us we are the apple of God's eye, the center of His attention. In what ways have you experienced the careful attentiveness of God? In what ways has God seemed to have lost sight of your needs? How difficult is it for you to trust God when it seems like He isn't answering your prayers?

7. Have you ever had to choose to quit being angry at God? What effect did your forgiveness have on your relationship with God?

8. The author says God's ultimate protection is the Resurrection. Do you believe that? Why? Why not? How can this realization give you confidence to trust God in difficult days?

9. How do you try to balance your sense of God-given ability with the call to be absolutely dependent on God? In what ways do you think God expects you to do your part? In what ways do you think God wants you to rest in His ability to provide?

10. What are you dealing with right now that is creating challenges greater than you feel you can handle on your own? How is God helping? What lessons is this time teaching you?

11. The author says true safety comes through obedience. Do you agree or disagree? Why?

12. The author says the people talking to Jesus in John 6 were "standing in front of the Manna of heaven and were asking for bread!" In what ways have you underestimated God's ability to provide for your need? Have you ever asked God to provide something you later realized you didn't need? What would you tell someone who is frustrated with God's apparent slowness in providing a solution?

Finish the prayer below:

Lord, I am learning to trust You above every resource in my life. As I am trying to live out my trust in You this week, help me . . .

Chapter 4 Questions

1. How difficult is it for you to trust God when He only provides enough for today? What is most difficult about obedience during days of scarcity?

2. In what ways do people tend to base their sense of identity
on their ability to accumulate "stuff"? Why do you think this
is so tempting?

3. How do you respond to God when finances get tight? Do
you tend to accuse God of abandoning you? In what ways do
these times draw you closer to God?

4. Has God ever asked you to sacrifice something? How difficult was it for you to obey His call? What lessons did you
learn through the experience?

5. The author says God's "blessing is reserved for those who
have abandoned their worship of 'stuff.'" Do you agree or
disagree? Why?

6. Have you ever experienced a time when God provided more
than you could have imagined? What were the lessons God
was teaching you? In what ways were you tempted to shift
your trust over to the blessing?

7. Do you agree that living in scarcity doesn't mean God is not blessing? What would you say to those who suggest a lack of material abundance is a sign of a lack of faith?

8. Have you ever been tempted to limit your obedience to God based on financial considerations? What was most difficult for you about this time?

9. If we really believed that God, not our wealth, was our source of blessing, what would change in our lives? How would we handle our money differently?

10. Have you ever been tempted to demand that God provide the resources you need *before* you follow His plan? Why do you think we have so much trouble following God into times of uncertainty?

11. Have you determined how much you need financially to meet your needs and take care of your family? What do you think God could do through you with the excess blessing He sends to you?

Finish the prayer below:

Lord, help me to be willing to follow You when You provide just enough for today. It is most difficult for me to follow You when I am lacking an abundance of . . .

I am confessing my tendency to need physical blessing before I trust You. So this week help me . . .

Chapter 5 Questions

1. On a scale of 1 to 10 with 1 being "not at all" and 10 being "completely," how comfortable are you with the idea that God might lead you into difficulty in order to build your character? Why?

2. What are some of the trials God has used to transform your life? How are you better today because of those difficulties?

3. When trials come, what do you think is the most difficult part of maintaining your faith? How do you handle this?

4. The author suggests that peace comes *before* the miracle. What do you think he meant? Have you ever experienced this?

5. When does God's discipline feel like a good thing? Why do you think this is true? What would you say to someone who is resisting God's discipline in his or her life?

6. The author says, "I love that God is going to transform me but hate that it is going to hurt." In what ways does God's work in our lives hurt? How do you get past the pain to see the joy of His work in your life?

Finish the prayer below:

Lord, I know You want me to be more like You, and that means You will lead me through difficult days. As I go through those kinds of days, help me to . . .

Chapter 6 Questions

1. Do you tend to interpret dependency on God as something to be enjoyed or to be endured? Why?

2. When does dependence on God feel risky? How do you get beyond the tendency for self-protection?

3. The author suggests that dependency on God becomes sweet when we take steps of faith because of what God can do, rather than because of what we can do? Have you ever experienced one of these decisions? What were the circumstances? How did God have to come through for you? What was the outcome? How did this experience strengthen your faith?

4. The author says, "When we choose to believe our success rests in God's ability, we can lose the fear and experience peace." Do you agree? Can you think of examples in your own life when this has been true?

5. How do you feel about the fact that whatever land God calls you to conquer will always be possessed by giants? What are some of the giants God is helping you defeat?

6. Manna is sweet because it allows us to transfer our faith to the next generation. What lessons will the next generation learn from watching your spiritual journey? What would you tell them is of the utmost importance?

7. If manna becomes sweet when we acknowledge difficulties as an opportunity for a miracle, what opportunities for miracles are you currently experiencing? How are you dealing with the emotions associated with desperate need? How can you reinforce an attitude of expectation during these times?

8. The author says, "We face our giants by recounting the many ways in which God's provision has proven sufficient." In what ways has God proven His ability to come through on your behalf? How do these memories help you during the difficulties you currently face?

9. The author says, "The cost of an easy life is far too great." What do you think he meant? Do you agree? Disagree? Why?

Finish the prayer below:

Lord, I am learning that dependence on You is a sweet experience that leads to peace. As I am learning to trust You in the days ahead, help me to . . .

Chapter 7 Questions

1. Why do you think some people are transformed by adversity while others are crushed by it?

2. When you think of the current generation of believers, do they remind you more of the parents who left Egypt, or their children who entered Canaan? Why?

3. In what ways does the need for "abundance" distract people from obedience to God's plan in their life? What is most difficult about this for you personally?

4. The author says we can no longer tolerate partial obedience in our lives. Where do you struggle most with this? In what ways is God calling you to a spiritual transformation of obedience?

5. Look back at the seven commitments of a transformed heart (pp. 118-20). Which one is most difficult for you? Why? How do you need God to help you deal with this commitment?

6. The author suggests the Holy Spirit has to bring the transformations we need. In what ways are you trying to "manufacture" these transformations in your heart? Take a few minutes and ask God to do in your heart what you cannot accomplish on your own.

7. In what ways do you see the value system of our culture, the thirst for more and more, impacting the church? What do you think God would say to us about this?

8. What was your reaction to the author's teaching on tithing? How could tithing deepen your faith? What is most difficult for you about this biblical standard?

9. How do you find Sabbath in the middle of difficult days? How do you respond to God when you haven't had time to stop and find spiritual nourishment? How will you create times of spiritual refreshing in the days to come?

Finish the prayer below:

Lord, I commit to stay faithful to You whether You lead me into days of plenty or days of want. As we walk this journey together, help me to . . .

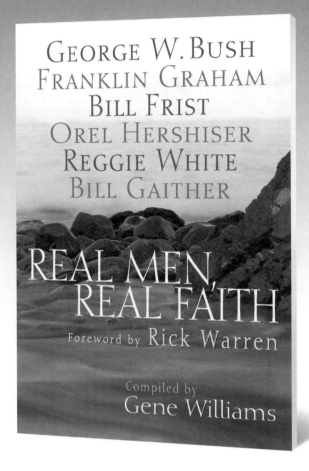

ALSO AVAILABLE FROM BEACON HILL PRESS

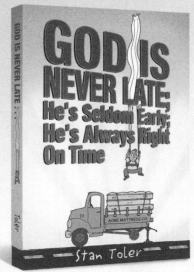

God Is Never Late; He's Seldom Early; He's Always Right On Time is about trusting God even when it seems He is running late. In an entertaining and insightful style, Stan Toler re-

978-0-8341-2105-8

minds us that God has perfect control over the events of our lives—and that He has the power to order those events in a loving, meaningful way. Despite our anxiousness, impatience, and worry, God is faithful to work in our lives at just the right time. He'll never be late.

God Is Never Late; He's Seldom Early; He's Always Right On Time
Stan Toler

Also available from Stan Toler
God Has Never Failed Me, but He's Sure Scared Me to Death a Few Times
The Buzzards Are Circling, but God's Not Finished with Me Yet

BEACON HILL PRESS
OF KANSAS CITY

BECOME A SERVANT WHO
LEADS WITH SIGNIFICANCE

Join Nehemiah, a remarkable man of God, on a journey of leadership
that matches the trials and challenges leaders face today. Through his story, you'll
recognize the difficult task of balancing the promises of biblical leadership with
the premises of secular leadership and learn how Nehemiah was able to serve with
full integrity in both of these settings. Practical exercises, Scripture references,
illustrations, and relevant examples make this book a great resource for pastors,
church leaders, teachers, business professionals, or leaders of any kind.

Becoming Nehemiah: Leading with Significance
By David L. McKenna
ISBN: 978-0-8341-2217-8

Available wherever books are sold.